A Teton Country Anthology

A TETON COUNTRY ANTHOLOGY

Edited by Robert W. Righter

ROBERTS RINEHART, INC. PUBLISHERS

For Trisha and Bonnie

May they and their generation enjoy
and preserve the mountains

Contents

Acknowledgments

A PROJECT of this nature is not an individual activity. Invariably friends, collegues and even strangers contribute, sometimes unknowingly. To those anonymous persons who sparked ideas in visitor centers, campgrounds or perhaps even on river rafting trips I extend my thanks. To interested and helpful friends and colleagues such as Leigh Ortenberger, David Love, Ken Diem; I hope my selections reflect your wise council. I also owe a debt to National Park Service historian John Daugherty and Grand Teton Natural History Association head Sharlene Milligan. They not only provided photographs, they made many helpful suggestions, and gave constant encouragement. Robert Rudd of the Jackson Hole Museum and Bobbie Taylor of the Teton County Historical Society both deserve my thanks for their willingness to share their knowledge and their collections. I must also say that although Jackson is a small town, Nancy Effinger and the Teton County Library staff are unsurpassed in finding esoteric materials and providing a quiet place to use them.

I would be remiss without acknowledging the opportunity to spend five wonderful weeks at the University of Wyoming/National Park Service Research Center on Jackson Lake; an inspirational place to work, although the stunning view of the Teton Range from the library served as a major distraction! Also, this project would not have been completed without continued support of publishers John Schwartz and Rick Rinehart who never wavered in their support of this book. Carrie Jenkins merits special mention for editing my often unruly prose.

Lastly, Sherry L. Smith deserves my sincere thanks. My wife, my friend, and a historian to boot, we work well together in all things, and this small collection represents her thoughts and effort as well as mine.

Introduction

JACKSON HOLE and the Teton mountain range are perhaps un-matched in alpine beauty. Each year millions of Americans draw inspiration and renewal through visiting this diverse region of nature's handiwork. Now, as in the past, persons viewing the range close at hand—or even at a distance—are at a loss to express their wonder. Language does not seem adequate. Per-haps the views are indescribable? Comparisons have been useful: Billy Owen, credited with the first ascent of the Grand Teton, called the peak the "Matterhorn of America." Visitors before and since have favorably compared the range with the European Alps. Charles D. Walcott, writing officially in 1898 for the United States Geological Survey, called the Teton country the "Switzerland of America," and foretold that tourists would find the Tetons, Jackson Lake, and Yellowstone "the grandest trip . . . to be found anywhere." Few today would question the truth of his prediction.

The purpose of this anthology is to present the reader with a sampling of some of the finest writing on the region. However, it also seeks to give a historical feel for the Teton country. We continue to be fascinated with the past and with those who wrote and experienced a fresh and pristine country. Thus I have selected works which are gracefully and lucidly written, but which also reflect the history of the "Hole."

The Teton country was among the last regions to reveal itself to the American people, thus its history is a recently written one. A few fur trappers and miners were familiar with the country in the nineteenth century, but they recorded little, and what they wrote was considered suspect. Jackson Hole was north of the great immigration route to California and Oregon. Railroads spanned the continent to the south, and eventually the north, but never through Jackson Hole. It was an admittedly beautiful country, but minerals were scarce, timber was inferior, farming proved impossible, and cattle ranching was marginal. With its isolation and lack of exploitable resources, settlement was slow in coming.

The earliest accounts of Jackson Hole can be attributed to its proximity to Yellowstone and its superb hunting and fishing. Those who came to Yellowstone often were lured south to the Tetons. Nathaniel Langford and James Stevenson (Hayden Survey, 1872) fell into this category, as did George Bird Grinnell (Hague Survey, 1884) some years later. President Chester Arthur toured Jackson Hole on horseback on his 1883 visit to Yellowstone. Well-heeled sportsmen intent on killing big game include the genteel Englishmen William A. Baillie-Grohman and Sir Rose Lambert Price, Theodore Roosevelt, and Earnest Thompson Seton and his young wife, Grace Gallatin. They all found exceptional hunting, but much more.

These people came as visitors—encountering the mountains, woods, and sagebrush-covered plains, and writing of their noteworthy experiences—and then moved on. Others had a more intimate, long-standing association with the valley. Author Owen Wister (*The Virginian*) first came to Jackson Hole in 1885 and returned occasionally until his death in 1938. When his family joined him they often stayed at the JY Ranch, the first dude ranch in Jackson Hole. Guest ranches featured a close but comfortable relationship with nature appealing to an upper class that could afford to travel and spend a month or more in semi-primitive leisure. Some of the best accounts of the Teton country come from "dudes"; ranch visitors who felt the beauty of the country, and could articulate those feelings through the written word. Fannie Kemble Wister, Owen Wister's daughter, fondly recalled her youthful equestrian summers of 1911 and 1912 spent at the JY Ranch.

The Teton country story, however, is more than one of visitation and description. It has a dramatic human history, one of homesteading, grit, and pluck to gain a living from a land of harsh climate and stingy resources. Frances Judge's grandparents homesteaded in the valley, and in her essay she tells of the pioneer life, quite different from that experienced by the affluent, but not without its joys and awareness of living in a special place.

As settlement increased, wildlife decreased. Most affected by the increased human population were the elk. Winter starvation and death was often their fate in the early years of the twentieth century. Rancher/guide/photographer Stephen Leek recorded the tragedy for the nation with his pen and lens. The result of his work was the beginning of protection through the establishment of the National Elk Refuge, a permanent feature of the valley today.

Settlement threatened not only the elk, but the whole pristine look of Jackson Hole. Some residents favored development, while others argued that northern Jackson Hole should be free of human imprint. The controversy took different forms, but perhaps the hottest was the fight to establish Grand Teton National Park. For over thirty years the forces of private property and public conservation collided in varying degrees of intensity. Most pioneer residents agreed that the pristine beauty of Jackson Hole ought to be preserved. They disagreed on how and who should do it. Many could not accept that the nineteenth-century atmosphere must be preserved by a twentieth-century bureaucracy. Olaus and Margaret Murie were in the midst of this epic conservation battle. Passions were fervent and families were sometimes at odds. As the Muries put it, "there was no such thing as getting together and talking it over."

Today most everyone agrees that the establishment of Grand Teton National Park in its present size represents a victory for both the nation and the local economy, but the means used to create the park can still inflame emotions.

One reality that is not debatable is the resplendent Teton mountains. The range forms a focal point for all eyes, with its over powering scale and inspiring variety of light and shadow, snow and rock. People of imagination and literary skill have composed much, but perhaps no one has surpassed Fritiof Fryxell. He not only viewed the mountains, he knew them through countless hikes and climbs. His description concludes the anthology.

Selecting the most pertinent and interesting essays on such a popular topic as the Teton country must inevitably force hard choices. I have attempted to bring together a group of essays by well-known Americans and Englishmen that not only tell us about the early Teton country, but do so with style and grace. Hopefully what follows will give the reader an accurate idea of the Teton country landscape and its history, and do so in a fashion that says: "read on!"

Robert W. Righter
Jackson Hole, Wyoming
Summer, 1989

PART ONE

EXPLORING THE COUNTRY

Nathaniel Langford
The Ascent of Mount Hayden

Although the Greater Yellowstone region was known to Indians and white trappers and miners, it was not until the 1870s that the region was systematically explored and publicized. No person was more instrumental in the effort than Nathaniel Langford. He was the leader of an expedition in 1870 to Yellowstone, an exploration that inspired Ferdinand V. Hayden to lead a scientific expedition in 1871. In 1872 Yellowstone National Park was created, with Langford as the first superintendent.

Hayden returned in 1872 instructing his trusted assistant James Stevenson to explore Jackson Hole and the Teton mountains. Nathaniel Langford accompanied the Stevenson party, as did William Henry Jackson, who photographed the landmark mountains for the first time. The following account of their explorations of the country south of the Yellowstone was prepared by Langford for Scribner's Monthly *and centers on their climb of the Grand Teton, or Mount Hayden, as this exploration party named it. Although subsequent evidence indicates that Langford and Stevenson were unsuccessful in reaching the summit, this account nevertheless conveys the excitement and peril of mountain climbing with nothing more than a rope and raw nerve.*

OUR ASCENDING party, fourteen in number, being fully organized, we left camp at 10 o'clock, on the morning of the 28th July, and followed up the cañon nine miles, to the spot chosen for our temporary camp. Here we rested, and dined; after which

The Stevenson-Langford party camp in Teton Canyon in July of 1872. It was from this camp that the assault on the Grand Teton was launched. *American Heritage Center, University of Wyoming*

Messrs. Adams and Taggart ascended a mountain on the left of the camp to a plateau, 3,000 feet above it, from which they were able to determine the general features of the route to the base of the Grand Teton. That peak rose majestically in the distance above a hundred smaller peaks, its sharp sides flecked with snow, and its bold gray summit half buried in fleecy clouds. It was indeed the lord of the empyrean. Pressing on toward it, they ascended a point of the plateau separated by an intervening chasm of nearly a thousand feet in depth from the elevation over which their pathway lay. The setting sun admonished them that they had barely time to return to camp before dark. They reached there in time to join the boys in a game of snow-balling, a singular amusement for the last days of July.

At half past four the next morning, the thermometer being 11° above zero, the party was aroused, and after partaking of a hearty breakfast, each man provided with an alpine staff, and a bacon sandwich for mid-day lunch, departed from camp, intent upon reaching the topmost summit of the loftiest Teton. The first two miles of the journey lay directly up the cañon, and over countless heaps of fallen trees. This tedious course of travel only terminated to give place to another, still more wearisome, through a ravine, and up a steep acclivity which we were enabled only to ascend by clinging to the points and angles of projecting rocks. Pausing at the summit to take breath, we saw lying between us and the first icy ridge a vast field of snow. Our aneroids showed that we were 9,000 feet above the ocean level—a height which entirely overlooked the walls of the cañon we had ascended, and took in an immense view of the surrounding country. Far as the eye could reach, looking northward, peak rose above peak, and range stretched beyond range, all glistening in the sunbeams like solid crystal. In the immediate vicinity of our position, the eye roamed over vast snow-fields, rocky chasms, straggling pine forests, and countless cascades.

The snow-field over which we next traveled, instead of the smoothness of a freshly-covered plain, was as irregular, as full of hummocks and billows as the rocks beneath it and the storms which for years had swept over it could possibly make it. It presented the appearance of an ocean frozen when the storm was at its height. Clambering over the first ridge, we traveled on in the direction of the second, which obstructed our view of the Tetons. Our route was over huge bowlders alternated with snow, and at this hour of the morning, before the sun had visited it, no traveling could be more unpleasant. We found our alpenstocks of infinite service, and we may thank them for the many falls we escaped upon the slippery surface, as well as for the comparative safety of many we made. Two miles of this kind of exercise brought us to the second ridge, which was composed of crumbling rock, and at least six hundred feet above the level of the field we had passed over. The view from this point was magnificent, but almost disheartening, from the increasing obstruction it presented to our progress. Another stretch of snow, rising to a sharp ridge, lay in front of us, at lease five miles in length, across which, in our line of travel, was another upheaval of crumbling rock. On our right, a thousand feet below, was the open, blue Lake Cowan.

Resuming labor, some of our party crawled around the side of the gorge, preferring rather to cross over the snowy ridge on our left, than to descend the slippery side of the elevation upon

which we stood. Several projecting ledges of crumbling rock lay between them and the snow, from which, as they passed over them, detached masses rolled down the bank endangering the lives of all below. Mr. Beckler, by a sudden jump, barely escaped being crushed by a large rock, which whistled by him like an avalanche. As he jumped he fell, and rolled down upon an out-cropping bowlder, receiving an injury which disabled him. Others of the party slid down the ridge unharmed, and encountered fewer difficulties in their journey along its base than its sides. The snow in the long ridge was at least two hundred and fifty feet in depth, and apparently as solid as the granite it covered. After a walk of more than a mile upon its glassy surface, we made a long descent to the right, and passed over a lake about 600 yards long by 200 wide, covered with ice from twelve to fifteen feet thick. There was nothing about this frozen water to indicate that it had ever been open. The ice which bound it, as well as the snow surrounding, seemed eternal. So pure and clear

The Stevenson party (Hayden Survey) in Jackson Hole in 1872. This William H. Jackson photograph is one of the first taken of the Teton Range. *American Heritage Center, University of Wyoming*

was this frozen surface, that one could see, even at its greatest thickness, the water gurgling beneath. At the distance from which we first saw it, we supposed this lake lay at the very base of the Tetons, but after we passed over it, there still stretched between us and that point two miles of corrugated snow. Still receding and receding, those lofty peaks seemed to move before us like the Israelites' pillar of cloud, and had we not seen this last snow-field actually creeping up to the top, and into the recesses of that lofty crest, from which the peaks shoot upward to the heavens, we should most willingly have turned our faces campward from the present point of vision, and written over the whole expedition, "Impossible."

There is no greater wonder in mountain scenery on this continent, than the tendency it has to shorten distance to the eye and lengthen it to the feet. A range of mountains apparently ten miles distant may be fifty miles away. A plain, to all appearances as smooth as a floor, is often broken into deep ravines, yawning chasms, and formidable foot-hills. Everything in distance and surface is deceptive.

Beyond the lake we ascended the last rocky ridge, more precipitous than the others, to take a last look at the dreary landscape.

We seemed to be in the midst of an arctic region. All around was snow and rock and ice. Forward or backward everything was alike bleak, barren and inhospitable; but our great labor was still unperformed. Encouraged by the certainty that we were upon the last of those great snow environments which lay at the feet of the mountains, we pushed onward to the base of the immense saddle between them. At this point several of the party, worn out with the day's exertions, and despairing of reaching the lofty summit which still towered five thousand feet in mockery above them, abandoned all further effort. Our kind surgeon, Dr. Reagles, had considerately accompanied us to the base of the ridge, provided with instruments and bandages in case of accident.

We lost no time in selecting from the numerous ravines that were made by the erosion of the friable rock from between the ascending granite ledges, such an one as we believed might be traversed to the top of the ridge without meeting lateral obstructions. Some of our party, mistaken in this, encountered when midway up the side a precipitous wall of granite, which made their return imperative. Five only of the company, after clambering over a snow-slide a thousand feet or more in width, reached the depression upon the right of the Grand Teton which we called "The Saddle." The ascent thus far had tested the endurance of all who made it. It was only difficult or dangerous to those who had selected the wrong passage through the ledges. We ate part of our luncheon while upon "The Saddle," which we reached about noon, and rested there a quarter of an hour beneath the shadow of the Great Teton. It seemed, as we looked up its erect sides, to challenge us to attempt its ascent. As we gazed upon the glaciers, the concavities, the precipices which now in more formidable aspect than ever presented themselves to us, we were almost ready to admit that the task we had undertaken was impossible to perform. The mountain side, from the Saddle to the summit of the Grand Teton, arose at an angle of sixty degrees; broken by innumerable cavities and precipices.

MOUNT HAYDEN AND MOUNT MORAN—FROM THE WEST.

Our leader, Captain Stevenson, had pushed on ahead, and when Messrs. Hamp, Spencer and the writer had reached "The Saddle," he was far up the mountain, lost to view in its intricacies. Our fears concerning him were allayed by occasionally seeing his footprints in the débris. Very soon after we commenced the ascent, we found ourselves clambering around projecting ledges of perpendicular rocks, inserting our fingers into crevices so far beyond us that we reached them with difficulty, and poising our weight upon shelves not exceeding two inches in width, jutting from the precipitous walls of gorges from fifty to three hundred feet in depth. This toilsome process, which severely tested our nerves, was occasionally interrupted by large banks of snow, which had lodged upon some of the projections or in the concavities of the mountain side,—in passing over the yielding surface of which we obtained tolerable foothold, unless, as was often the case, there was a groundwork of ice beneath. When this occurred, we found the climbing difficult and hazardous. In many places, the water from the melting snow had trickled through it, and congealed the lower surface. This, melting in turn, had worn long openings between the ice and the mountain side, from two to four feet in width, down which we could look two hundred feet or more. Great care was necessary to avoid slipping into these crevices. An occasional spur of rock or ice, connecting the ice-wall with the mountain, was all that held these patches of snow in their places. In Europe they would have been called glaciers. Distrustful as we all were of their permanency, we were taught, before our toil was ended, to wish there had been more of them. As a general thing, they were more easily surmounted than the bare rock precipices, though on one occasion they came near proving fatal to one of our party.

Mr. Hamp, fresh from his home in England, knew little of the properties of snow and ice, and at one of the critical points in our ascent, trusting too much to their support, slipped and fell. For a moment his destruction seemed inevitable, but with admirable dexterity he threw himself astride the icy ridge projecting from the mountain. Impelled by this movement, with one leg dangling in the crevice next the mountain side, and the other sweeping the snow outside the glacier, he slid with fearful rapidity, at an angle of forty-five degrees, for the distance of fifty feet, falling headlong into a huge pile of soft snow, which prevented his descent of a thousand feet or more down the precipitous side of the mountain. I saw him fall, and supposed he would be dashed to pieces. A moment afterwards he crawled from the friendly snow-heap and rejoined us unharmed, and we all united in a round of laughter, as thankful as it was hearty. This did not quiet that tremulousness of the nerves, of which extreme and sudden danger is so frequent a cause, and underlying our joy there was still a feeling of terror which we could not shake off. Pressing carefully forward, we attained a recess in the rocks, six hundred feet below the summit, where we halted.

While resting here, far above us, we heard the loud shots of Captain Stevenson, which we answered. Soon he joined us, with the information that he had been arrested in his ascent, at a point two hundred feet above us, by an intervening rock, just too high for him to scale. It was perpendicular, and surmounted by a wide sheet of ice stretching upward towards the summit, and covered with snow. He had made several ineffectual efforts to reach the overhanging edge of the rock, and at one time lost his foothold, his entire weight coming upon his hands while he hung with his face to the wall. It was impossible without a leap to reach a standing place, and by loosening his hold without one he would drop several hundred feet down the mountain. Fortunately, there was a coating of ice and snow, which reached midway from his feet to his arms, and into this, by repeated kicks with the toe of his boot, he worked an indentation that afforded a poise for one foot. This enabled him to spring on one side to a narrow bench of rock, where he was safe.

We had periled life and limb to little purpose, if the small matter of five hundred feet was to prevent the accomplishment of our task. We determined, therefore, to ascend with Captain Stevenson, and make another effort to scale the rock. When I saw the perilous position from which he had escaped, I could not but regard his preservation as almost miraculous. In spite of nervous exhaustion, Mr. Hamp had persevered in the attempt to

LOOKING OFF FROM THE SUMMIT OF MOUNT HAYDEN.

climb the mountain, but as all upward progress from this point was extremely hazardous, he and Mr. Spencer were persuaded to avail themselves of a foot-hold in the rocks, while Captain Stevenson and I made a last essay to reach the pinnacle.

A rope which I had brought with me, cast over a slight projection above our heads, enabled me to draw myself up so as to fix my hands in a crevice of the rock, and then, with my feet resting on the shoulders of Captain Stevenson, I easily clambered to the top. Letting the rope down to Captain Stevenson, he grasped it firmly, and by the aid of his staff soon worked his way to my side. The shelving expanse of ice, overlying the rocky surface at an angle of 70^0, and fastened to it by slight arms of the same brittle material, now presented an obstacle apparently insurmountable. Beside the danger of incurring a slide which would insure a rapid descent to the base of the mountain, there was the other risk, that the frail fastenings which held the ice-sheet to the rocks might give way while we were crawling over it, and the whole field be carried with us down the terrible precipice. But the top was just before us, not three hundred feet away, and we preferred the risk to an abandonment of the task. Laying hold of the rocky points at the side of the ice-sheet, we broke with our feet in its surface a series of steps, up which we ascended, at an angle deflecting not more than twenty degrees from a vertical line, one hundred and seventy-five feet, to its topmost junction with the rock.

The peril to which this performance exposed us was now fully revealed, and had we seen it at the foot of the ice-sheet, the whole world would not have tempted us to the effort we had made. Why the entire mass of ice, yielding to our exertions, was not detached from its slender fastenings and hurled down the mountain is a mystery. On looking down through the space which separated it from the rock, I could see a half a dozen icy tentacles, all of small size, reaching from wall to wall. Seemingly the weight of a bird would have loosened the entire field. We felt, as we planted our feet on the solid mountain, that we had escaped a great peril—and quenching our thirst from one of the numerous little rivulets which trickled down the rock, set resolutely at work to clamber over the fragments and piles of granite which lay between us and the summit. This was more tedious than difficult, but we were amply rewarded when, at three o'clock P.M., after ten hours of the severest labor of my life, we stepped upon the highest point of the Grand Teton. Man measures his triumphs by the toil and exposure incurred in the attainment of them. We felt that we had achieved a victory, and that it was something for ourselves to know—a solitary satisfaction—that we were the first white men who had ever stood upon the spot we then occupied. Others might come after us, but to be the first where a hundred had failed was no braggart boast.

The several pinnacles of the Grand Teton seen from the valley seem of equal height, but the inequality in this respect was very apparent at the top. The main summit, separated by erosions from the surrounding knobs, embraced an irregular area of thirty by forty feet. Exposure to the winds kept it free from snow and ice, and its bald, denuded head was worn smooth by the elemental warfare waged around it. With the unshorn beams of a summer sun shining full upon us, we were obliged to don our overcoats for protection against the cold mountain breeze. Indeed, so light was the atmosphere, that our respiration from its frequency became almost burdensome, and we experienced, in no slight degree, how at such an elevation one could at a single exposure suffer the opposite intensities of heat and cold. Above the ice-belt, over which we had made such a perilous ascent, we saw in the débris the fresh track of that American Ibex, the mountain sheep,—the only animal known to clamber up the sides of our loftiest peaks. Flowers also, of beauteous hue, and delicate fragrance, peeped through the snow, wherever a rocky jut had penetrated the icy surface.

On the top of an adjacent pinnacle, but little lower than the one we occupied, we found a circular enclosure, six feet in diameter, composed of granite slabs, set up endwise, about five feet in height. It was evidently intended, by whomsoever built, as a protection against the wind, and we were only too glad to avail ourselves of it while we finished our luncheon. On entering it we found ourselves a foot deep in the detritus, which had been worn by the canker of time from the surrounding walls. The great quantity of this substance bore evidence to the antiquity of the structure. Evidently the work of the Indians, it could not have been constructed less than a century ago, and it is not improbable that its age may reach back for many centuries. A period of time which human experience cannot calculate, was required to produce this wonderful disintegration of solid granite. It was the great wonder of our day's work, and proved that even the Indians, usually so incurious, had some time been influenced by the same spirit which had inspired us. No such curiosity, I imagine, affects the Indians of our day. The toil and exposure of a scramble up the Teton would daunt the bravest of them, if he should happen to possess energy enough to attempt it. Better men than any that now belong to the North Western tribes, must have ascended this mountain, and left this evidence of their visit: but what motive save that of the merest curiosity or a trial of skill could have caused the ascension, it would be impossible to determine.

Far away on the northern horizon, scarcely distinguishable from the clouds with which they are intermingled, we saw the Belt, Madison and Main Rocky ranges, from which long, lateral spurs stretch down on either side, and close up the immense amphitheater by uniting with the Malade Range on the south. Within this vast enclosure, and more immediately beneath us, we overlooked the valley of the Snake, the emerald surface of Pierre's Hole with its mountain surroundings, the dark defile leading into Jackson's Hole, and Jackson and De Lacy lakes, Madison Lake, the source of the Snake River,—Henry's Lake, the source of the North Fork, and afar off, beyond these, the cloud defined peaks of the Wind River mountains, and the peaks surrounding the great lake of the Yellowstone. Our elevation was so great that the valley beneath us, filled as it was with knobs and cañons and foot-hills, had the appearance of a vast and level plain, stretching away to, and imperceptibly blending with the distant mountains.

We gazed upon the varied beauties of this wondrous panorama until reminded by the position of the sun that we had scarcely time to effect our descent, and return to camp before dark. Great caution was necessary while passing down the ice belt lest it should become detached, but it was our only passageway to the bottom, and we were greatly relieved when we reached in safety the cranny occupied by Hamp and Spencer. At this point Captain Stevenson separated from us, and was the first to reach the base of the mountain. We clambered over the rocks and precipices with all possible expedition, and stood in safety upon the saddle, just as the sun was setting.

The interval between sunset and evening in these high latitudes is very brief, and we had yet to descend the ridge. In our haste to accomplish this we selected a pathway between ledges too abrupt to scale, which led directly to a precipice, thirty-five feet in height, at the base of which was a mass of granite fragments and debris from three to four feet deep. We were now in a dilemma. Either we must pass the declivity or re-ascend the steep mountain side, five hundred feet or more, and select another passage. Crawling to the edge, I saw at a distance of twenty feet a jutting point, which would afford standing room for a single person, and about eight feet below it, a smaller projection, too sharp on the face for a safe foothold. Passing the rope alternately around the bodies of my comrades, I let them down the perpendicular wall to the base, then throwing the middle of the rope over a projecting crag, and seizing the two ends, I lowered myself to the narrow shelf first described, whence a well directed leap enabled me to poise myself on the smaller projection below, and gather for a final jump into a pile of debris, where my comrades stood. Our safe descent being thus accomplished, we had yet the snow-fields, ridges, and gorges to traverse, before we arrived in camp. Fatigued with the exercise of ascending and descending the Teton, the passage of these ridges was the most exhaustive effort of our lives. It was after nine o'clock, and very dark, when we first caught sight of our camp-fire, afar down the chasm. After a rough walk over prostrate trunks, through deep depressions, amid pine thickets, climbing bowlders, penetrating chapparal, wading streams,—at just thirty minutes past ten, when all our comrades had thought some serious and perhaps fatal accident had befallen us, we entered camp amid cordial greetings and shouts of delight. The joy of a re-union, after even so brief a separation, was as earnest and sincere as if we had been parted a year.

William A. Baillie-Grohman
Camps in the Teton Basin

William A. Baillie-Grohman was another of those privileged En-glishmen who found spice in life through travel and often perilous adven-ture. Contrary to some, however, he carried out his adventures with little of the trappings of aristocracy. When he came to Jackson Hole in 1880 he was twenty-nine and in the prime of his life. Traveling light, he hunted in the Wind River range, then continued north, entering Jackson Hole by way of the Gros Ventre River valley.

As a mountaineer who climbed extensively in the Tyrol country of the Austrian Alps, Baillie-Grohman made frequent comparisons of the Teton country with European alpine scenery. Above all, this blue blood revelled in the freedom of the West with its absence of artificiality so common in the society circles to which he was accustomed. He brought a hearty sense of adventure to his western escapade, and he had the ability to express that adventure and excitement in his prose. His account is not only eloquent, but an excellent expression of the hunter/naturalist/conservationist tradition which would eventually take hold in Jackson Hole.

THERE ARE few spots in the Western mountain lands around which there hangs so much frontier romance as about "Jackson's Hole," the trapper name for the Teton Basin. Few camp-fires in the wilds beyond the Missouri fail to thaw out of "oldest men" tales of that famous locality. When an unprecedented trapping feat has to be located, that mountain-girt Eden will be chosen by the narrator. If an impossible Indian fight has to be fathered on to some quiet and out-of-the-way nook, the "bad man" who tells you the story will make "Jackson's Hole" the bloody battlefield. If a great mining yarn goes the round, dealing with creeks paved with nuggets of gold, but to which somehow the first discoverer never could retrace his steps, the prospector invariably chooses for its site the Teton Basin. When I first became acquainted with the Land of the West, I had Teton Basin on the brain. Everybody seemed to have been there, or was going to visit it. And from the stories I heard, I soon came to the conclusion that it was, undoubtedly, an insufficiently wonderful camp-fireside tale about that region that called down upon the narrator, a beginner in Western Troubadouring, the deserved and well-known reprimand, "Young man, young man, ain't you ashamed to talk so, when there are older liars on the ground?"

All kinds of great hunters made me their confidant, and poured into my ears their personal experiences—how they had gone to the Teton Basin "dead broke," and returned with gold dust leaking out of their torn boots, and thirty horses doing their level best to pack out of their torn boots, and thirty horses doing their level best to pack all the beaver pelts along. "Jackson's Hole" soon became, in my eyes, a sort of beatified "home for destitute trappers." And to judge by the numbers who had been there, the place was apparently of good size to hold all the old mountaineers domiciled in it—and what was strangest, apparently for no other earthly reason than for the pleasure of living in the Teton Basin; for of course, with legions of the best fur-hunters after them, the poor beavers had vanished to haunts less favoured by those old, old—nay, the oldest trappers of the country, men who trapped the *Cache la Poudre* when Fremont was yet sucking his thumbs in the idleness of babyhood.

I well remember how puzzled I was on my first accidental meeting with Port—whom, as he was pointed out to me as one of the best trappers of the country, I was rather surprised to meet 500 miles away from that spot—my stock question to all old trappers, "When are you going back to the Teton Basin?"

received the startling answer, "Never been there; and I kinder reckon few white men have." At the time I thought that was the very first "up-and-down" lie told me since crossing the Missouri; but somehow, as time went by, and the brilliant Paris green that coated my composition came off in big patches, I came to the conclusion that it was about the very first truth I had stumbled on.

In the subsequent two expeditions with him through other portions of the Rocky Mountains, bringing me into campfireside contact with many would-be "old men of the mountains," my notebook gradually became filled with *reliable information* on different routes to that sequestered spot—and I certainly never knew a place have so many "*best* ways to get there." Singular to say, when, on our third and present outing, we made it our goal, the nearer we got to the spot the fewer grew the travellers who had spent either their youth, or their prime, or their old age in that trapper's paradise; and when finally, in July, 1880, we passed Fort Washakie, the nearest post and the nearest human habitation to it; we found that there was actually not a single person there who knew the way to it, or who had ever been there. An absent scout was said to have actually visited it; but he was away, and for the rest of the 180 or 200 miles across the Great Divide we were our own Teton Basin discoverers.

A few words will suffice to indicate its locality. South-West of the Yellowstone Park, it lies on the boundary of Wyoming and Idaho, between the Teton Range and the Grosventre Mountains. Up to 1881 it was very difficult of access, being enclosed on all sides by mountain ranges that were very little known, and could only be crossed at certain points, over which led Indian trails known only to a very few white men. But the wonderful tales of the quite exceptional natural beauty of the spot, circulated by the few who had visited it on their lonesome fur-hunting expeditions, had taken root, and spread in the remarkable manner already indicated. Up to 1879 only large, well-armed expeditions (the one Government Exploration Party, under the renowned Professor Hayden, had touched it in 1872), or trappers who, by taking Indian wives, had become Indianized, could venture to enter that country, for the two Indian tribes—the Nez Percés and Bannacks—whose hunting-grounds it was, were then very hostile. The Indian war of 1878 cleared them out, and when we visited the basin in 1880, we had the whole country to ourselves. With two exceptions, I saw not a single white man from the end of July to the end of November, and for three months of that period saw also no Indians. Today access is made easier, for the narrow-gauge Montana line, branching off Northward at Ogden, passes Fort Hall, from whence Jackson's Hole can be reached from the West in seven or eight days' travel over Indian trails.

We reached the confines of the Basin on a beautiful September morning. Debouching very suddenly from a deep canyon, to a high knoll overlooking the whole of it, we happened to strike the most favourable point from whence to view the mountain-girt paradise spread out before us.

At our feet lay the perfectly level expanse, about eight or ten miles broad, and five-and-twenty in length. Traversing the basin lengthwise, we saw the curves of the Snake River—its waters of a beautiful beryl green, and apparently as we viewed it, from a distance of five or six miles, of glassy smoothness—winding its way through groves of stately old cottonwood-trees. A month or two before, the Snake had inundated the whole Basin, and the grass that had sprung up retained its bright green tint, giving the whole picture the air of a splendid trimly-kept old park. Beyond the river the eye espied several little lakes, nestling in forest-girt seclusion under the beetling cliffs of the boldest-shaped mountain I am acquainted with, *i.e.* the Grand Teton Peak, rising in one great sweep from an amazingly serrated chain of aiguille-like crags sharply outlined against the heavens, and shutting in one entire half of the basin,—the other semicircular enclosure being the mountain range on which we stood. It was the most sublime scenery I have ever seen.

Many of the Colorado mountains are called the Matterhorns of America—with about as much justification as the more diminutive Ben Nevis, or Snowdon, merits that name. With the Teton it is, however, different; for it makes, so far as I know, the only and very brilliant exception to the usual dome-like

For William Baillie-Grohman and those who followed, such as this proud hunter, a bull elk was a grand prize. *American Heritage Center, University of Wyoming*

formation of the Rockies. In shape it is very like the Swiss master-peak; but inasmuch as the Western rival rises in one majestic sweep of 7000 feet from this natural park, to an altitude all but the same (13,800 feet), I would, in this instance, in point of sublimity give the palm to the New World.

Pursuing the hardly perceptible Indian trail (we came along the Grosventre Creek) which zigzagged down the steep slope, we soon reached the level bottom of the Basin, and shortly before sundown made, in one of the extensive groves on the banks of the Snake, what, without exception was the most strikingly beautiful camp of my various trips. The immediate surroundings were of idyl-like charm. From the smooth sward, fresh, and singularly free of all rubbish, rose straight and massive the stately cottonwoods, their trunks of a silvery sheen, while festoons of creepers connected garland-like, often at great altitude, the upper branches of the trees that formed the grove. Immediately in front of us glided the broad river, its glassy surface broken here and there by a minute swirling eddy. Right at the bank it was ten or twelve feet deep; and great salmon trout, each spot discernible, hovered under the abrupt rootwork bank. Not a sound was audible, not a sign of living being was visible. The river was not broader than sixty yards, and trees as large as the ones that surrounded us dotted the opposite bank. Over this mass of brilliant verdure rose the Titanic Teton; and did we not know that two miles of level ground intervened between us and the base, the clearness of the Western mountain air is so deceptive that the great Peak seemed to grow right out of the opposite grove. Bend your neck as far as you would, still your gaze seemed incapabale of reaching the needle-shaped summit, and—similar to the old Californian miner, who when he first saw El Capitano, in the Yosemite, said it took two looks to get squarely to the top of the peak, with a chalk-line to mark off on the cliffs how far his first had got—the real sublimity of its height impressed itself only after the second or third look, notwithstanding that Nature came to our aid by substituting a narrow belt of snow-fields half way up the mountain for the old Californian's chalk-mark.

For once, as we all stood crowding the bank, feasting our eyes on the scene, I wished myself alone, to do homage to what I then, and still, consider the most striking landscape the eye of a painter ever dreamt of, by half an hour's examination more in keeping with the wonderful stillness which cast a further charm over it. For once, too, two of the unimpressionabale Western characters round me gave vent to appreciate exclamations; the third, however, young Henry—a hopelessly matter-of-fact be-ing—turned sublimity into ridicule, by his "Darn the mountains! Look at those beaver dams yonder." Alas! I have given up all hope to teach that young mind to admire; and I believe that were he suddenly introduced into Olympus, the only feeling that would move him would be expressed in a terse "Doggarn it, if I ain't forgotten the traps and the pison."

The following morning we crossed the Snake at one of the upper rapids, where two of us, and several of the horses, got sound duckings, and the dogs and one colt were swept down stream, amid considerable commotion, for quite a quarter of a mile. An hour's ride across the level brought us to the banks of one of the two larger lakes I have spoken of, and where, as the sequel will show, I had some unique fishing.

Let me say a few words on the topic of old Walton's gentle art in the Rockies.

The light in which the Express-wielding Englishman, in quest of sport in the Far West, appears to the frontiersman, the rough-and-ready resident of those equally rough-and-ready regions, is sufficiently quizzical to establish in their eyes our national claim to something more than oddity. Still more incomprehensible to the Western "boy" is, however, the Englishman who visits those districts for fishing, or, to use names by which that art is known to him, for *lining, poling, bug-hooking,* and a series of other equally unflattering designations. Most English shooting parties visiting the United States for sport take back with them trophies of the chase, more or less numerous according to the means of transportation employed by them while out in the wilds. These heads, horns, and skins are at least something tangible; and though the question frequently asked of me, "How much them ar' hides and headgear be worth over in the old parts," proved to me that it would be useless to try to dispel the deeply rooted suspicion that my much-treasured bear skins, wapiti, and big-horn heads were intended for vulgar sales and mart; they are nevertheless "something that shows," something that in another world and among another people may possibly be worth certain, if limited, number of dollars.

Much worse does the fisherman fare who visits the semi-civilized home of those intensely practical roving forerunners of civilization. The fisherman, poor fellow, has nothing more tangible to take back to his home than pleasant recollections and an astonishingly big score, both about balancing each other for utter valuelessness in the frontiersman's eyes, both betraying, in his opinion, about the same degree of lunacy in a mild shape. No sane man, argues the free but dollar-hunting citizen of Uncle Sam's empire, rich enough to pay for the men, horses, and the stores of the outfit, could possibly act so strangely; leave his "tony" house, discard the luxuries of civilization—"turning his back on whiskey," is his own expressive phrase for similar conduct—put up with all the discomforts and hardships of camp life, which to him have of course long lost all charms; and all this—after travelling five or six thousand miles, and spending enough money to start a silver-mine—for what? To stand all day in water knee-deep and "line" fish!

So thinks the Western man while he gladly pockets the guide's fee, or the hire for the horses and mules that have carried you and your belongings to the scene of your big bags. His quizzical gaze rests upon your elaborate fishing-tackle; the five-guinea rod, or spy-glass pole, as I have heard it called, is to him as wonderful an instrument as your parchment book of flies, the pride of your art, is of mysterious use and purpose. Landing net, reel, and all the numerous etceteras usually to be found hovering about the person of Walton's disciples, are not less puzzling to him; and when finally he sees you issue forth from your tent arrayed in all the brand-new finery of your West-end outfitter, his mouth puckers up more than usually as he squirts from it a stream of tobacco juice. He will not say much, for the Western man is apt to keep his impressions to himself; but he will think all the more. *His* fishing has been done in a different style. A change of diet becoming desirable, his ponderously heavy Sharp's rifle or the keen axe—its shape and make a *chef-d'oeuvre* of practicalness—is laid or flung aside, while the next patch of willows furnishes him with a rod, not as long or as straight as yours, but strong enough to handle a five-pound trout, or a lazier salmon of twice that weight. His line will not break—of that we can be assured, for it is a very cable among lines, being fine-cut buckstring (cut from Indian-tanned buckhides); while the hook, fastened to one end by a knot nearly as big as a pea, is of home manufacture, old horseshoe nails, well hammered, being favourites for the purpose. For bait, the Western fisherman is never at a loss; if a "bug"—all insects go by that name, grasshoppers and crickets being favourites—cannot be found, a piece of raw meat, the iris of the last deer he killed, or a minnow will do. If the time of day be propitious, the sky clear, and no ripple on the water (these conditions I have found to be of the greatest moment), the native angler will land in half an hour as many trout as he can conveniently carry. If bugs are scarce, he will cut thin long slices from the first fish he catches, the glittering scales being, after insect bait, the most deadly for the finny tribe. Often have I watched such fishing on lake, river, and creek. The gigantic hook, duly "spiked" with an equally huge green or black "hopper"—both so large that I once wagered (and won) I could pick off the bait with my rifle at a distance of thirty steps—splashes down into the circling eddy, and often before it has time to reach the bottom a two-pounder will be testing the strength of the buckskin line, which, if the "pole" does not give way, would hold a fish ten times his weight.

I am no fisherman; in fact all the trout I had ever caught up to that period could be easily stowed away in the pockets of my shooting-coat; so before I write any further, and betray my ignorance on some vital point, as I assuredly should, I am desirous of impressing this fact upon the reader.

When leaving Europe I found that a light fishing-rod that had been knocking about my gun-room, unused for years, could be crammed into one of my rifle cases; and passing down Oxford Street on the day preceding my departure, I favoured the owner of one of the many fishing-tackle-making emporiums in that thoroughfare with a general order to put up ten shillings' worth of line and trout fly hooks. This personage; more astonished I suppose at the nature than pleased by the meagre extent of my patronage, did so in the most business-like (*i.e.* prompt) manner, never deigning to lose a further word upon such a customer.

I was glad of it at the time, for had he asked me any one of the ninety-nine questions regarding details—which I believe are necessary to define the exact nature of the fly you want—he would have been no doubt shocked beyond measure by the extent of my ignorance. Subsequent events, however, made me regret my carelessness in the selection of the tackle; for my very first day's fishing demonstrated to me in the most convincing manner that in my unskilful hands the line was far too light, the flies useless, and the hooks themselves hardly strong enough to hold a half pound trout. At a rough calculation that day's fishing cost me nine shillings and elevenpence worth of tackle; for at the termination I found myself minus most of my hooks, the greatest part of my line, and the two top pieces (the spare one being one) of my rod snapped in two; and of the countless fish that had risen to my bait, none landed but the very smallest. Fort Washakie, the last human habitation we had passed, was 180 or 200 miles east of us; and where to get a fresh supply of line and hook nearer than the post, I knew not.

Games just then was very scarce; the Bighorn were still high up on the mountains, and Wapiti had not yet come into the Basin, so that we had been out of meat for one or two days; and the long face of my men when, on my return to camp from my first day's fishing, I informed them that I had sacrificed nearly all my hooks and part of my rod, put a hungry aspect on the matter, our "grub outfit" being then of the very lightest description. My pocket tool-box—a very essential commodity, as I found out, without which nobody ought to travel in those regions—had unfortunately been *câched* with some extra stores and the tent a week or so before, and hence we could not metamorphose horseshoe nails, of which we had some few with us, into fishhooks. But the instinct of practical self-help, so strongly developed by Western travel, came to the rescue, and by the end of a couple of hours' work, aided by the bright light of a huge camp-fire, we had completed three very deadly instruments. One was a landing net made of the top of a young pine-tree bent into a hoop, with an old flour sack laced to it with buckstring, half-a-dozen holes being cut in the canvas to let out the water. This was a triumph in itself; but what will the reader, who is probably an expert fisherman of long experience, say when he hears of the other two? I had just six hooks left, and the broken top pieces of my rod (I must plead ignorance of the technical name of the component parts of a rod) furnished the necessary thin thread wire to make two hooks out of six, by fastening three together, their points diverging grapnel fashion. The torn pieces of line were carefully twisted into a stout hawser, the strength of which we tested by fastening it to the collar of a Newfoundland pup, and lifting him clear from the ground.

The next day was a warm balmy September morning—not a cloud was to be seen in the sky of Alpine blueness. I returned to the same spot on the banks of the lake—the scene of the whole-sale robbery of hooks on the preceding day, and on my way thither filled a small tin canister with "bugs" in the shape of remarkaby live crickets, of large size and jet black colour, that could be found in thousands on the open barrens. In an hour I had landed about forty pounds of trout, mostly fish about two pounds in weight. All the larger fish—and I must have had at least three times the number on or near my hook—broke away; while the very large ones—of which I saw quite a number, and some of which must have scaled six pounds or seven pounds—snapped up the bait *en passant* in the most dexterous manner.

My favourite spot for the sport was, as I have said, at the outlet of one of the lakes (Jennie's Lake it is called on the latest Government Survey map), and the time an hour or so before sunset, when, after a long day on the rocks and in the dense timber, I would have returned to my old horse and got on my way back to camp. Highly fantastical, not to say demented, must I have appeared to an Old World angler, as, wading old Boreas into the water where creek and lake joined till it reached within a foot or so of the saddle, he would stand perfectly motionless till I had filled the two capacious Stalker's bags slung one on each side of him with the speckled beauties. Sitting well back in the saddle, with both legs dangling down on the same side, my rifle slung over my back—the landing net when not in use hung on one of my steed's ears, the only handy place for it—I plied my grapnel with neverfailing success. Fish after fish, with hardly a quarter of a minute between, would gobble up the bait, gener-ally still alive, and if the fish was not of large dimensions, would be jerked out of the water, and safely ensconced in the folds of the flour sack.

As I have said, I usually began fishing "an hour by sun"—the trapper expression for an hour before sunset, and, with only one exception, I succeeded in filling the two bags with twenty-five pounds or so of fish (while proper tackle would have accomplished it in a quarter of an hour or twenty minutes) before the long shadows of the tall pine-trees growing down to within two or three feet of the water's edge would fall across the smooth, glassy surface of the tranquil mountain tarn. The sun once off the water, the fish would vanish as if by word of command, and I do not remember to have caught a single in the lake after sundown. Resuming my usual seat in the saddle—a signal well understood by trusty Boreas, and with a yelp of delight from the young Newfoundland, who, intensely interested in the whole proceedings, would sit, all attention, on the bank fifteen or twenty yards off, restrained only by my word from keeping up constant communication between me and the shore—I would turn my horse's head campward. Once, and only once, did serious disaster threaten me—it was when a more than commonly vigorous two-pounder snapped the threefold gut. But luck stood by me, and the second throw with my spare grapnel landed the very criminal, the hook still in his jaws.

Has the reader ever eaten salmon trout (for I believe this is the proper name of the fish I caught in the Teton Basin) fried in bear fat, with a bit of beaver's trail simmering alonside the pink mess? If he has not, I venture to say he knows not what makes a right royal dish.

Three times a day did six big frying-pans full appear on our primitive greensward dinner-table, and never did fish taste nicer, and never did four men and two dogs eat more of them. Hardly credible as it sounds, thirty pounds a day was hardly sufficient to feed our six hungry mouths; and when, towards the end of my short stay in the Basin, great economy in flour became imperative, forty pounds vanished in a similar wonderfully speedy manner.

Two ludicrous little incidents happened to me in the Teton Basin; and though I took, to use Western parlance, a *back-seat* in both, I shall narrate them. The first one occurred in this way: I had filled an old tin to the brim with hopper-bugs, and was crossing the outflow of the lake, seated, or rather crouching, on Boreas's back, with legs tucked under me so as not to get them

Baillie-Grohman, the Chester Arthur party and many other early visitors followed the Gros Ventre River into Jackson Hole. *American Heritage Center, University of Wyoming*

wet; when right in the centre of the stream, with the water up in the saddle, my steed took it into his head to come to a dead halt. My impressive "Git up!" was in vain, and considering my ill-balanced position, and that my hands were filled with the "pole," landing-net, rifle, and bug-tin, while the reins were hanging knotted over his neck, it was not the easiest thing to enforce these words by more active measures. Just below me was a large deep pool, and as Boreas had a wonderful faculty of doing the most unexpected things when left to his own free-will, I dreaded a dousing in the limpid depth at my side. Tucking my rifle under my left arm, clutching the rest of my outfit in the same hand, and the landing-net in my teeth, I began to belabour his plump back with the thing most handy, *i.e.* the bug-tin. One whack, two whacks, and with a click out flew the bottom of the cannister, and for the next second it rained black bugs. Nearly all, of course, fell into the rapid-flowing stream, and the next instant were whirling for a brief second over the surface of the limpid pool. That moment, reader, I saw more fish than I had ever seen before or ever will see again.

The other little mishap was quite as ludicrous. I must mention that these bugs are lively animals. They jump, dodge about, and creep out of your way with astonishing rapidity, and the only manner I could stalk them successfully was to throw my limp felt hat at them with sufficient force to stun without squashing them. Even this requires some quickness and undivided attention. Well, one or two days preceding the above incident, I was out on my usual preliminary bug stalk; and going along with bent form, now hitting, then again missing, my plump game, my whole attention being fixed upon my occupation, I reached a clump of dense service-berry bushes. I had just delivered a successful throw, and was about to stoop to gather in the prize, when out of the bushes, as if growing from the earth, there rose—a grizzly. Rearing up on his hind legs, as they invariably do on being surprised, he stood, his head and half-opened jaws a foot and a half or two feet over my six foot of humanity, and hardly more than a yard between gigantic him and pigmy me. The reader will believe me when I say he looked the biggest grizzly I ever saw, or want to see, so close. It would be difficult to say who was the more astonished of the two, but I know very well who was the most frightened. My heart seemed all of a sudden to be in two places; for had I not felt a big lump of it in my throat, I could have sworn it was leaking out at a big rent in the toes of my moccasins.

Now grizzly shooting is a fine healthy sport—I know none I am fonder of; but there ought to be neighboring trees to facilitate *centralization to the rear,* and above all I must be handling my old "trail stopper"—and that moment I was here on a treeless barren, *en face* with one I "was not looking for," or "had not lost;" and yonder, 100 yards off, lay that famous old rifle—Boreas in the distance putting some spare ground between him and that noxious intruder. Fortunately the Old Uncle of the Rockies had more than probably never had anything to do with human beings, for I saw very plainly that he was more puzzled as to my identity than I was regarding his. His small, pig eyes were not very ferocious-looking, and first one, then the other, ear would move; expressing, as I interpreted it, more impatience than ill-feeling. I do not exactly remember who first moved, but I do recollect that on looking back *over my shoulder* I saw the old gentleman actually running away from me! On regaining possession of my rifle, which on this quite exceptional occasion I had allowed to get beyond my reach, as it interfered with my "buggings," I felt considerably braver, and spent the rest of the day in a vain endeavour to resume our acquaintanceship on more satisfactory terms. But the old gentleman evidently thought he had frightened me sufficiently, and so kept out of my way.

This is not the only bear story I could tell, but as none have the slightest claim either to originality or sensational adventure, I will not weary the reader's patience with what has been told so often, namely that grizzlies want no fooling.

A very cursory examination of Jackson's Hole ripened in us the determination of wintering in the basin, notwithstanding that we were quite alive to the fact that once a passage over the Main Divide was made impassable by the deep snows of winter, (we had twice to cross the great backbone at altitudes over ten and nearly eleven thousand feet,) escape from the basin was impossible for eight months, till the following July or August, for the two great rivers we had to cross are, on account of the melting snows, quite impassable during the spring. It was very fortunate that ultimately we were prevented executing this plan. I subsequently heard, too, from a trapper—the only human being who, so far as I could learn, had ever wintered in it—that owing to the sheltered position, enclosed on all sides by high mountains, and the altitude of the Basin itself (nearly 7000 feet), the snow remains lying, and is not blown off, as on the equally elevated plains, by the high winds. He told me—and I have every reason to believe him, for we found sufficient evidences that snow lies there very deep—that for three months the roof of his log cabin was flush with the white pall, and that he fed his three pack animals with elk meat, and bark of the cottonwood-trees boiled to a pulp.

We stayed for ten days in the Basin, and probably would have remained another fortnight had not a great forest fire, raging in the timbered regions north of us, the smoke of which we had seen for a week, threatened to invade the Basin, obliged us to leave it—with the intention, however, of returning a month or six weeks later. As it turned out this was not to be; and our winter palace, the site of which was duly selected, and the way to it blazed by me on the trees of the forest that shut it in, is yet to be built. Most annoying was one of the consequences entailed by the fire, namely, that I was prevented ascending quite to the summit of the great Peak. On one of my expeditions after the mythical mountain goats—which I can assure sportsmen are *not* to be found on the Teton Range, though on a chain about 120 miles north of it they *have* been killed—I got within 1000 or 1100 feet of the top; but the distance to the summit from our camp was too great to go and return in one day, and as no horses could be got further up than our camp, I decided to let the men help me to convey the necessary food, robes, &c., wherewith to pass a night or two close up to the summit. The men just then were very busy, and I unfortunately delayed the expedition from day to day, till the fire, running before a north-westerly breeze, and approaching us very rapidly, though yet several miles off, obliged us to leave the Basin by the way we had reached it. From the point which I reached on the main Peak, and from the top of a minor aiguille which I ascended, I could see what remained of the main ascent. Indeed had it not been so late that day, or had I been provided with some covering for the night, I would have proceeded there and then. And very sorry I am I did not, even without covering; the night I would have had to pass on the rocks would not have been the first in such a position. The remaining portion, as I had every chance to observe, was fairly easy for anybody trained to Alpine, and especially rock work. Many a second class peak in the Dolomites, though of lesser altitude, presents much graver obstacles than those that I saw on the uppermost portion of the Teton—the very formation of rock speaking for an easy ascent, while the snow was nowhere of exceptional steepness, and withal in perfect condition. In this respect I was rather disappointed, for the very bold outline of the whole mountain led me to expect a first class climb, though in point of distance the clearness of the air led me to underestimate it.

One of the chief difficulties in exploring the Teton Range, are the immensely deep canyons that cut up the chain in detached blocks. The water in many cases has worn them down to the level of the basin, and they are often so narrow that you come upon them with startling abruptness, and look down yawning gorges two and three thousand feet deep, and at the top only half that width. They are undoubtedly finer than anything we have in the Alps.

While in the Teton Basin we had a full moon, and if the reader cares to entrust himself to such a moonstruck individual, I shall ask him to accompany me on a quiet, after-supper stroll in the beauteous calm of night. Of the many nocturnal rambles I have enjoyed in the Rockies, the one in question stands out in pleasant relief, for the surroundings were exceptionally picturesque.

Our camp, pitched on a great spur of the Teton Range, two or three thousand feet over the basin, commands an expansive view, and even the bright lights of a huge post-prandial campfire can hardly outvie the brightness of night. About us there are half a dozen veteran spruce, so gnarled and weather-beaten as to resemble that grand tree of the Tyrol, the arve, its branches festooned with wavy tresses of the grizzly, "beard of the Alps." Supper, the pleasantest meal of the day, is over. The usual campfire conversation, dealing with recent events in our primitive travel, and mainly centering on sporting subjects, of late represented by my sorely disillusioned hopes of finding moose or mountain goats on the Teton Range—for the mountains were pictured to us by persons to whom even Port gave credence as harbouring great numbers of both species—has duly seasoned the meal.

We have lingered longer than commonly over it, and as usual

Henry has neglected to put the camp-kettle with the dish-
washing water on the fire, so that when finally it is remembered, and the much-travelled pot is placed near the blaze, the
circumstance is seized as a welcome excuse to lengthen that
luxurious after-dinner *dolce far niente,* while another outrageously
Western story, another hearty laugh, enliven our comfortable
repose. A glance at the "dipper," for some months our only
watch, for the two with which the outfit started have long been
invalided, warns me that it is time to set out, for the constella-
tion slants to nine o'clock, and there is half an hour's walk to the
sight of my, or rather our, stalk. I say "stalk," for such a moonstruck ramble as we intend to take would seem the height of
ridiculous sentimentality to the men, whose natures—good and
fine fellows as they are—are of the genuine frontier stamp, *i.e.*
up and down practical and unimpressionable. To save appearances, it is therefore advisable to let on such occasions a stalk
serve as an excuse for prolonged absence at strange hours.

The rifle is taken as a matter of habit, for here you never let,
or ought to let, it get beyond your arm's reach. You sleep with it
under your saddle pillow; when you fish, it is slung over your
back; and in the same way that in many of the missionary
churches in frontier-country the men stroll into church their
rifle in their hand, you would, so accustomed do you get to
handling your shooting-irons, very likely in a similar case do
precisely the same, or only discover what you are about to do, as
you are passing the doorstep. Not that I think there would be
any special harm about it—certainly no more than there is in
frantically gripping a tightly-rolled umbrella in the bellicose
"Who are you?" sort of fashion which distinguishes many a
brave son of Albion, as with squared shoulders he strides into
some peaceful Midlandshire church at home.

So, with the old "trail stopper" over our shoulder, we stroll
forth. A rise in the ground presently shuts out all view of the
camp, but 100 yards further on we again catch sight of the bright
pile, and the dark shadowy forms hovering about it. To the
uninitiated they would appear to be engaged in some mysterious
heathen rite, for while one is kneeling on the ground with his

face to the fire, his hands pressed to his breast, moving to and fro
in silent incantation; another is lying on his back, with one leg
held up high in the air; and the third is cutting mad capers in
front of the blaze. We know better; there is nothing at all
mystical about it. The first is drying a tin camp-plate he has just
washed, by pressing it against his body and rubbing it with the
cloth, much as had he a mild pain below his belt; the second is
testing the strength of his evening's handiwork, a new bridle,
plaited of long strips of elkskin; while the third has very probably burnt his fingers when reaching for the camp-kettle standing
near the fire.

We follow the slope dotted, with great boulders, leading us to
a lower level, and presently reach a buttress of rock, from which
en passant we see the Teton Basin stretched out at our feet—one
or two little lakelets, and the silvery coils of the great river
traversing the valley, reflecting the rays of the moon. We see
the whole vast slope of the Teton chain on which we are; for the
spur juts far out, enabling us to view not only the mountains
opposite, but also those that overshadow us. We see where great
profound canyons cut down in the massive range, and form
gorge-like fissures of extraordinary abruptness and depth.

Yonder dark streak, a few hundred feet over our heads, is
Timberline. In gentle curves it follows the spurs and the smaller
ravines that scar and fissure the face of the great chain. Beyond
the plainly-marked band, much of the rock is mantled by a pall
of glistening white, from which, in one great glorious sweep,
rises a huge black tooth, boldly outlined against the grey blue of
the nocturnal heavens. It is, as I need hardly say, the Grand
Teton.

The outline of the landscape is of entirely Alpine character.
Only in details does it differ. In daytime the searching glare of a
brilliant sun, cloudless skies, and a crystal atmosphere, give it a
tinge of crude disharmony. Peaks do not float in the air, for, so
to speak, there is no air that we can see or feel. The absence of
moisture in the atmosphere, while it affords vision far greater
play than in other mountainous landscape, is practically achro-
matic. The bold buttresses and pinnacles, their snow, their shad-

owy ravines, their gloomy canyons, are displayed with tantalizing precision and uncompromising hardness. There is no tender play of colour, no harmonious perspective blending the near and the far. There are no great banks of airy silver-streaked billows to give depth to the picture, and to cast fairy shadows upon the mountain slopes; while the wondrous play of shifting light and shade caused by these fugitive exhalations—effects dear to the lover of Europe Alpine scenery—is sadly wanting. By moonlight these features of landscape beauty are no longer lacking. In autumn, when the days are warm and the nights are cold, filmy vapour not unfrequently rises after dark. The summits of the mountains near their glittering heads from gauzy clouds of it, while the subdued and silvery light of the brilliant moon is chary of invading the gorges and ravines. There is light, there is shade, there is tender perspective. The stark rocks and austerely colourless backgrounds are lost in mysterious half-distances, and an air of tranquil, romantic beauty is cast over scenery, which at other times chills you by its raw vastness.

In viewing spacious panoramic landscape in America, one generally finds that the eye rarely encounters specific points about it that leave a lasting impression. When on some future occasion one endeavours to reconstruct the picture, it is far more puzzling than had it been European Alpine scenery. The picturesque details about the latter, far more numerous and far more varied, can somehow, much more easily be remembered.

We proceed on our stroll. Not the whole great mountain side is clothed in its primeval garb. In an hour's stroll we notice at least five or six more or less extensive expanses of timber, every one of different age. Fire, caused by lightning, and windfalls, avalanches, and hurricanes have all been at work, and all have left their distinctive mark. We pass grassy slopes, dotted here and there with very old trees, gnarled and weatherbeaten, and not a few of crippled shape, which in days long past were spared by the snow avalanche that started from the heights above and swept away their brethren, leaving on its course Cyclopean boulders strewn about on the glade, and now as deeply imbedded in the soil as had they always been there. Our walk has brought us to the foot of walls of rock of vast height, for here the main chain falls off in one great precipice. Skirting along their base through occasional groves of spruce pines, we presently reach the mouth of one of the canyons. Striking through the mountains at a right angle, it has cut the chain very nearly in two, and its perpendicular sides are quite 2000 feet in height. A small stream, ludicrously insignificant in comparison with the great gorge its waters have made for themselves, issues from the buttressed gateway. A colony of beaver, who generations ago made this spot their home, have, by building dams across the stream a few hundred yards lower down, turned a couple of acres of ground right at the mouth of the gorge into a beaver-meadow—a perfectly level expanse of velvety turf, as smooth and silken, and as brilliantly green, as some favoured lawn at home. We are standing a yard or two from the open space, in the deep shadow of some pines which encircle it on all sides save those where the abruptly-rising cliffs bound it. The glade-like beaver-meadow is flooded by the broad mellow moonbeams that stream through the gigantic portals of the gorge as though it were an arched window in some ruined old abbey. On the glade move about a small band of Wapiti, the stags whistling their weird Aeolian music, the hinds and their more than half-grown progeny feasting on the juicy "aftermath" that invariably grows on the rich alluvial soil of these beaver-meadows, grasses that in hue and texture are very unlike the rank herbage commonly to be found in elevated mountain regions. We stretch ourselves under the sweeping boughs of a great pine, and from there watch the family life, the occasional angry thrusts delivered by indignant master-stags in chastisement of some impudent youngster who has dared to approach his hinds. Stags ramble off into the forest, and stags come—now approaching within ten yards of our hiding-place, then gradually fading away into luminous "Waldesduft," the poetic German name for the shrouding vapours of the forest. Not thirty yards from us there lie close together, two big antlers, shed probably last season, but already blanched to chalk-like whiteness. One of the stags, wandering idly over the glade, presently comes up to them, and the lordly animal, for some reason or other displeased by these relics of his race, lowers his head, and catching up on his brow-tines one of the branching horns, weighing probable twenty pounds, tosses it like a feather, sending it crashing into the pine covert twenty yards off. The second horn he does not touch; he has shown what he can do. Except the quaint call of him and his fellows—sounds for which there is little cause, for the fair ones they are so jealously guarding evince no intention of evading their masters' endearments—save this, absolute stillness hushes the scene. The moon has topped the great chain, and no other light but that streaming through the vast rock-bound gateway of the gorge reaches the spot. Never did forest scene breath more entrancing peacefulness. As we look up at the great orb, it seems as if she had shone from that spot for millions of years, and would continue for time evermore to tough up with silvery sheen the little glade and the group of stately animals dispersed over it. But, alas! what a rude awakening awaits that family of Wapiti! Where, less than two years ago, the nearest human habitation was ten or eleven days' ride off—longer than it takes the traveller from the Old World to reach the New one—there will be, or perhaps there is already, a mining town, and Texas or Oregon steers will roam where, from time eternal, was the home of our antlered friends and of our favourites the indefatigable constructors of dams and beaver-meadows, while the ubiquitous cow-puncher or stock-raiser, who is turning the vast West into one huge cattle-yard, to the utter extermination of game, will replace the lonesome old "stags," who with their Indian squaws passed many a profitable trapping season in this beautiful mountain retreat.

The *Associated Press*
President Chester Arthur's
Journey Through the
Yellowstone National Park
and Northwest Wyoming, 1883

Many presidents of the United States have visited the Teton country, especially in recent years, but the first was Chester Arthur, who traversed the region in 1883 when it was a roadless wilderness. Arthur's purpose in embarking on a grand escapade in the wilderness is rather vague, but generally he wished to escape from Washington, regain his health, relax with friends, fish, confer with some of the Indians of the region, and familiarize himself with a part of the United States that was little known to him or anyone else.

It fell to General Phil Sheridan to arrange a party of Indian guides, horse packers, and some seventy-five armed cavalrymen. Among the dignitaries were Robert Lincoln, Secretary of War; George Vest, Senator from Missouri; and John Schuyler, territorial governor of Montana.

At Green River, Wyoming the entourage debarked the Union Pacific Railroad and headed by spring wagons to the north. They passed South Pass City—not a city but an almost-abandoned town—and the deserted Camp Stambaugh. Soon they began the descent to the Wind River valley and the small town of Lander. There the "Great Father" met with the chiefs of the Arapaho and Shoshone tribes. The meeting was cordial and colorful, although little was accomplished save that Senator Vest was informed by the respective chiefs that the tribes were much opposed to the allotment of the reservation into 160-acre and eighty-acre parcels.

North of the reservation the party entered a virtual wilderness devoid of roads or telegraph wires. Communication was crude and reporters were banned. Without their own resources the Associated Press and newspapers relied on daily dispatches which were probably written by Lieutenant Colonel Michael Sheridan, the general's nephew, and Lieutenant Colonel James Gregory. Although censored and sanitized, the dispatches nevertheless give the reader a good sense of the journey, if not all the newsworthy detail. The following dispatches of August 16 to August 23, 1883 describe the party's descent down the Gros Ventre River and through Jackson Hole.

THE PARTY:
CHESTER A. ARTHUR, President of the United States.
ROBERT T. LINCOLN, Secretary of War.
PHILIP H. SHERIDAN, Lieutenant General.
GEORGE G. VEST, United States Senator.
DAN G. ROLLINS, Surrogate of New York.
ANSON STAGER, Brigadier General, United States Volunteers.
JNO. SCHUYLER CROSBY, Governor of Montana.
M. V. SHERIDAN, Lieutenant Colonel and Military Secretary.
JAMES F. GREGORY, Lieutenant Colonel and Aide-de-Camp.
W. P. CLARK, Captain, Second Cavalry, Acting Aide-de-Camp.
W. H. FORWOOD, Surgeon, United States Army.
GEO. G. VEST, JR., Saint Louis, Missouri.
ESCORT:
TROOP G, FIFTH CAVALRY, Captain E. M. HAYES, Lieutenant H. DeH. WAITE.

CAMP ISHAM, GROS VENTRE RIVER, WYO., *Aug.* 16, *via* FORT WASHAKIE, WYO., *Aug.* 18.—The President and party left Camp Lincoln, at Lincoln Pass, this morning at 6:30, and con-

Prominent members of the Chester Arthur party of 1883 pose for photographer F. Jay Haynes. Seated from the left are: John Schuyler Crosby, Governor of Montana Territory; Lieutenant-Colonel Michael V. Sheridan; President Chester Arthur; Robert T. Lincoln, Secretary of War; and George G. Vest, U.S. Senator from Missouri. *Wyoming State Archives, Museum, and Historical Department*

tinued the march down a tributary of the Gros Ventre and the main stream a distance of nineteen miles, going into camp at a grassy point on the main river, which has been named Camp Isham, in honor of the Hon. Edward S. Isham, of Chicago. Camp Lincoln was a beautiful spot, presenting to the eye, towards the east and north, all the grandcur of the Shoshone range of snow-clad mountains, and to the west and south the snow-capped peaks of the Gros Ventre range. Pines and tamaracks cover the base and lower lines of the ranges, opening at intervals into beautiful grassy parks.

The descent down the mountains to the valley of the Gros Ventre is rugged, but was accomplished by the President and party without accident, they only dismounting at one steep and difficult place. As we approached Camp Isham a depression in the range enabled us to get a view of the lofty peaks of the Teton range, at the base of which we expect to encamp to-morrow night.

Secretary Lincoln and Captain Clark, with two Indians,

started early this morning in pursuit of elk. They will render no doubt a good account by bringing into camp to-night the results of a fine day's hunt in a country which abounds in game.

The President and remainder of the party, by reason of both the exercise and rest which their grip had given them, are in fine condition, and are not in the least fatigued by their ride on horseback.

The weather is cool, the air delicious and invigorating, and the scenery grand.

GROS VENTRE RIVER, WYO., *Aug.* 18, *via* FORT WASHAKIE, WYO., *Aug.* 19.—At 6:30 a.m. the President and party mounted their horses and started from Camp Isham. We marched down the valley to the Gros Ventre about ten miles, and then crossed that stream to the north side. Thence the trail lay away from the river through cañons and over mountains of considerable elevation. At one point we wound round the precipitous side of a mountain, at the base of this nearly perpendicular bank, about 1,000 feet below, the green waters of the river rolled and tumbled and lashed themselves into a white fury. A stumble, and horse and rider would have gone headlong to almost certain destruction. Much of the country of this valley is rolling, the soil rich, and the grasses thick and nutritious. The Indians with us claim that the snow falls to great depths here in the winter, but there are evidences that game subsists itself in the valley at that season of the year. In olden times this region was one of the favorite winter camping-grounds of the Sheep-eater band of Indians, a branch of the Shoshones, who lived at all seasons near the snow, and subsisted mainly on the flesh of the mountain sheep or big-horn, which they hunted with dogs and killed with arrows and clubs.

The Sheep-eaters have been absorbed by the Shoshones and Bannocks, and now live at agencies, but their old trails can still be seen leading across mountains over which it would seem impossible to take their families and rude belongings. The latter were indeed poor, as they dressed mostly in skins and furs, cooked their meat over the coals and lived in the rocks and caves. One of our guides belongs to this band but he—an old man now—was a boy when his band gave up this peculiarly wild and savage life.

About fourteen miles out we rose to the crest of a high bluff, from which a most beautiful crescent-shaped little valley met our gaze. Somber pine-clad mountains to the left, at the base of which ran, swiftly and turbulently, the Gros Ventre River, to the right high hills of dark red argillaceous rocks, with here and there ravines filled with foliage; part way down their sides the short bunch grass commenced, thin at first, then thickening to almost a turf when it reached the little mesa below; beyond this some low-lying hills.

The beautiful blue sky above, the dark green mountains to the left, the rich red hills to the right, the russet brown grass of the valley, relieved here and there by the bright green willow bushes and small cottonwoods, the stream of pure cold water made a grand picture of an ideal camp, and with one accord the whole party voted to remain there over night. We rode down, and after our appetites, sharpened by exercise and mountain air, had been satisfied by a hearty luncheon, rods and reels were gotten in shape, and the entire party went fishing. Gen. Stager made the largest catch, Senator Vest next and the President third, but many of those caught by Gen. Stager were white fish, while those of the President and Senator were wholly trout. Enough fish were caught by the members of our party, not only for our own use, but for the soldiers, packers and Indians with us, all of whom had a fish feast. Capt. Clark returned this evening from a two day's hunt after elk and bear. He had but little success. All the party are well and enjoying the fishing, hunting, horseback exercise and mountain air with keenest zest. In honor of the President, Gen. Sheridan named this camp "Camp Arthur."

CAMP TETON, *Aug.* 18, *via* FORT WASHASKIE, WYO., *Aug.* 20.—Promptly at 6:30 this morning we mounted our horses, and not without longing, lingering looks behind, rode away from Camp Arthur. Our course was in a westerly direction, along the

north side of the Gros Ventre River. The air was clear and
bracing, and the day as fine as any with which we have been
favored since we set out from Fort Washakie. The trail was
beset with few of those difficulties with which our fortnight's
travels in the wilderness have made us so familiar. Indeed, in the
absence of fallen timber, rocky side-hills and steep ascents and
pitches, the ride would have seemed somewhat monotonous but
for a single feature which actually glorified it. We had climbed
to the summit of a long hill about five miles from Camp Arthur,
when there suddenly burst upon our view a scene as grand and
majestic as was ever witnessed. Below us, covered with grass
and flowers, was a lovely valley many miles in extent, through
which was threading its way the river on whose banks we had
just encamped. Along the whole westerly edge of this valley,
with no intervening foothills to obstruct the view, towered the
magnificent Teton Mountains, their snowy summits piercing the
air 13,000 feet above the sea level and 8,000 feet above the spot
on which we stood in reverent admiration. It was the universal
sentiment of the party that that sight alone would have fully
repaid all the toils and perils of the march. We are encamped in
the Teton basin on the bank of the Gros Ventre. The locality,
aside from the splendid views of the mountains which it affords,
is our least attractive camp. The river at this point has an excellent reputation as a trout stream, but the wind has been blowing
at too many miles an hour to permit much success in angling. It
has been powerful enough to break the ridge-pole of our mess
tent, but fortunately not beyond repair.

To-morrow we shall resume our march and expect to make
camp near the so-called Buffalo Fork of the Snake River.

Camp Hampton, On Snake River, *Aug.* 20, *via* Fort
Washakie, *Aug.* 23.—The President's party reached this camp
after traveling about eighteen miles along foothills between the
Shoshone and Teton Mountains. The camp is named in honor of
Senator Wade Hampton, who was expected to accompany the
party. Its location is grand, being on the banks of the Snake
River and facing the entire range of the Teton Mountains. Judge

Rollins shot and brought in his first antelope. Nearly all the party are engaged to-day in angling for trout, the President and Senator Vest outstripping the rest, and vying for supremacy. Each landed a two and a half pound trout from the bluff facing the camp, which feats were witnessed by the entire command. Their catch for the day is much larger than on any day during the trip. At our last camp the temper of all the party was severely tried by the extremes of weather experienced. Hot weather in the middle of the day, and severe gales of wind throughout day and night, accompanied with blinding clouds of dust. Ice formed one-half inch thick on water buckets standing before the tents during the night. To-day the weather is clear and bracing, and all the party are in perfect health. To-morrow's march will take us to near the southern boundary of the Yellowstone Park.

CAMP STRONG, WYO., *Aug.* 21, *via* BOZEMAN, MONT., *Aug.* 22.—Reveille call at 5 awoke us all from a refreshing sleep, though the ice in our buckets this morning was proof that three blankets had been none too many during the night for our comfort.

Half-past 6 found all the tents struck and packed on the mules, and the Presidential party in the saddle.

Our route to-day of thirty miles lay nearly northward over the foothills of the Shoshone Mountains, avoiding the marshy bottoms of the Snake River, which are very treacherous. It was a rough and rugged country, covered for nearly a quarter of the distance traveled by dense tracks of burned and fallen timber. At noon we reached a sparsely timbered knoll which commanded a view of Jackson's Lake, with the snow-covered Tetons rising from its shores in the background, which repaid us for our severe, hot and dusty march in the early part of the day.

The omniscient reporter who claims to be with us, and who has been purely a mythical personage since we left the railroad at Green River, carefully and considerately located the Secretary of War at Fort Washakie for an indefinite period after we had started on our present trip across the mountains, and as the

Secretary had never been absent, it is a matter of much curiosity as to how the inventive genius of this fictitious correspondent would be able to restore him to us. As a matter of fact, Mr. Lincoln has been one of the keenest daily observers of the resources of the country through which we are passing, and is constantly and pleasantly reminding us of his presence.

This evening we are camping at the crossing of Snake River, which was named last year, by Gen. Sheridan, Camp Strong. Our tents are pitched on the banks of the stream in a grove of lofty pines. Trout are abundant, an opportunity the party are taking advantage of, for it is their last for fishing before reaching the Yellowstone region. The surroundings of this camp are beautiful and the opportunity for sport so good that the President has decided that we remain here another day.

CAMP LOGAN, LEWIS LAKE, *Aug.* 23, *via* LIVINGSTON, *Aug.* 25.—The white frost was still thick on the blades of grass, leaves, shrubs and plants, and glistened in the morning sunlight like diamond dust, and the mists and vapors rested close on the surface of the river as the Presidential party mounted at 6:45 a.m., and started out for the day's march. Last night was the coldest we have experienced, being 20 degrees Fahrenheit at 6 a.m., and in the mess tent the water which had been served a few moments before the party sat down for breakfast formed a beautiful network of ice on the inner surface of the glasses.

The trail was very crooked to-day, and led over a low range of mountains covered with pine forests. At intervals we found open, grassy parks, but the most of them were only a few acres in extent. About twelve miles out we came upon the lower falls of Lewis or Lake Fork, a dark gray gorge cut through solid walls of volcanic rock, its sides nearly perpendicular. About 600 feet below us the stream rushed and tumbled over its dark bed, broken white by its fretting. The upper falls, some six miles from the lower, we saw at a distance through an opening in the evergreen trees; it seemed to drop from out the dark foilage behind it like a flood of lace. Five miles further on we went into

Captain Hayes and his staff enjoy a clear day and pleasant weather while accompanying the President through his sojourn in Jackson Hole. *Haynes Foundation Collection, Montana Historical Society*

camp in a lovely open park at the head of Lewis Lake, the only spot on the shore which is not densely timbered.

The camp has been named Logan, in honor of the Senator, who was to have been one of the party, and whose unavoidable absence we have all regretted. Our tents look out on this beautiful sheet of water. The sound of the swirl of the waves on the beach mingles pleasantly with its twin sister sound, the soughing of the winds in the trees near by.

Along our line of march to-day we saw large quantities of Indian tea, diminutive species of evergreen whortleberries five to ten inches high, found only in timber and at an altitude of from 8,000 to 10,000 feet. The Indians are fond of the tea made from the dried leaves and stems of this plant, and I have been told by those who have drunk it that it forms a pleasant substitute for our own.

Yesterday we remained at Camp Strong, and its surroundings are worthy of more than a passing notice. A grassy bottom surrounded by mountains clad with evergreens, trees of all sizes from the young seedling up to mature age, scattered singly, grouped in clusters, or massed into dark forests. Our tents were pitched on the banks of Snake River, which here possesses all the attributes of a first-class trout stream. Clear, pure water rippling over pebbly bottoms, with here and there swift currents, eddies and deep holes. The President and Senator Vest, our two most expert fishermen, made the best of our stay, and scored the greatest victory yet achieved over the finny tribe.

At one cast the President landed three trout, weighing in the aggregate four and one-quarter pounds, and at each of some six other casts took two fine specimens. The President secured the greatest weight, the Senator the largest number, the total weight being 105 pounds. The sport is now about over. Senator Vest has caught the largest trout during the trip, it weighing three and one-half pounds.

Looking back over our course from Fort Washakie, where we first mounted our horses, abandoned wheeled vehicles, and took the Indian trail which has led us through some fertile valleys, across some bad lands, and over rugged mountains, many memories linger pleasantly in the mind of every member of the party. The hailstorm at Camp Crosby, the dust which sifted in our tents at Camp Teton, the trials of fallen timber, are lost and forgotten in the pleasant associations of the rest of the journey.

Picturesque Camp Lincoln, with its banks of snow lying placidly and slowly melting near the trail, and near the snow flowers, which had all the freshness of early spring, tender forget-me-nots, wild asters, buttercups, columbines, the latter with a delicate and scarcely perceptible shade of blue in its rich white, and for which many deem it the most beautiful of the wild flowers found in the Rocky Mountains, a carpeting of scarlet and blue and bold; added to this the White Mountain flox, nestling close to mother earth, and in such profusion as to suggest the idea that the hand of Nature had grasped some of her myriad stars and scattered them in wanton profusion on the grassy slopes of this romantic region.

Camp Arthur, grand beyond the power of pen to describe, located in a bend of the Gros Ventre River, and looking down upon it from the crest of the hill over which the trail led, we also got the first good view of the royal Tetons, or Titans, as they should be called. To the west forests of pine and spruce mantling the mountains. To the south and east clay and sand stone rising high in the sky, and rich red from its iron coloring, masked here and there by green foilage. The short, thick grass of the little valley furnished splendid grazing for our animals, and the trout, within twenty feet of the tents, made the immediate surroundings most delightful. Then the Teton basin, large as the state of Rhode Island, and covered at this season of the year with nutritious grasses, and profuse in evidences of being the winter grazing grounds of antelope, deer and elk. The near future must practically determine its value for stock purposes. Then Jackson's Lake, as we saw it from the crest of a high bluff on our line of march, a gigantic sapphire, its surface fretted and blown into white-caps by the winds which swept down over Mount Moran, and moanings lost themselves in the gloomy forests beyond.

Nature has indeed given a royal setting to this jewel, twelve miles long, three miles wide—on the east and north a fringe of quaking aspen and willow brush, on the west and south spruce and pines clothing the feet of the grand Tetons and scrambling up their sides until vegetation dies out. Above this the fissures and chasms of the grim, gray pile of rocks, filled with snowbanks, some of them 3,000 feet deep and of dazzling whiteness in the sun. Yes, the scenery along our route will furnish many pleasant memories in the years to come.

William Owen
The Matterhorn of America

William O. Owen, a professional surveyor headquartered in Laramie, Wyoming, roamed the Rockies at the turn of the century. Mountaineering was his passion, and by the time he was thirty, he was familiar with the peaks of the Uinta Range, the Rabbit Ears Pass area of Colorado, the Big Horn Mountains, the Wind River Range, and most of the lesser ranges of the northern Rockies.

Owen's reputation, however, is linked to the Teton Range. Leigh Ortenberger, today's most knowledgeable historian of climbing in the Tetons, has stated that "there is perhaps no name better known in association with the Teton Range of northwestern Wyoming than William Octavius Owen, 'Billy Owen of the Tetons'." Such a tribute is based upon the fact that Owen was a member of the three-man Franklin Spalding party, the first party to indisputably scale the Grand Teton in 1898. Until his death in 1945, Owen claimed the peak as his conquest, and was so successful that the closely associated Mt. Owen was named in his honor.

He wrote a great deal about the Tetons, but much of it was colored by his obsession to discount Nathaniel Langford's 1872 claim of the first ascent of the Grand Teton, which does not make for engaging or inspirational reading. However, Owen was a talented writer, and in 1891 he was free of crusades. In that year he, his wife, another couple, and a guide unsuccessfully attempted the climb. Later he published this account of their adventure in Frank Leslie's Weekly.

IN THE northwest corner of Wyoming, about twenty-five miles south of the Yellowstone National Park, from a range of rugged and perpetually snow-clad mountains whose christening dates back some seventy-five years, rise three of the grandest peaks in North America. They are known as the Three Tetons, and are mentioned in Irving's "Captain Bonneville," and by the renowned pathfinder, John C. Fremont, in his official report to the government covering his exploration.

These three peaks, by name, are probably more familiar to the tourists who have visited this Western country than any others in the entire Rocky Mountain system and yet I believe it perfectly safe to assert that they are in reality as little *known* as the giant snow-clad summits of equatorial Africa. The reason for this latter fact is readily to be found in the great difficulties that must be encountered in reaching them—difficulties that can be overcome only by excess of nerve and first-class physical endurance.

From the west, these peaks are easily seen two hundred miles distant, and viewed from this point they are seemingly as sharp as needles. The summits lie in a northeast and southwest direction and are almost exactly a mile asunder. The farthest north of the three is known as the Grand Teton, and has an altitude of 14,150 feet; the other two rising respectively 13,400 and 13,100 feet above the sea. These figures were obtained from careful transit and barometrical measurements and are the means of twenty independent observations.

They are truly Alpine in character and in this respect, if in no other lie entirely without the realm of comparison with other North American peaks. That the loftiest of the three has not yet attracted the attention of the mountaineering fraternity is little short of wonderful, for it possesses every feature that gives life and charm to mountain climbing.

The Grand Teton bears a marked resemblance to the famous Matterhorn of the Old World, as seen from the Riffel, and has many physical characteristics in common with its far-famed prototype. In one respect, at least, it surpasses that celebrated mountain. The Matterhorn from its base rises about five thou-

William Owen as a young man. Although Owen worked as a surveyor and was an accomplished photographer, from an early age mountaineering in the Rocky Mountains was his first love. *American Heritage Center, University of Wyoming*

sand feet, while the Teton, on the east side, lifts its head 7,500 feet above the valley at its immediate base, in a smooth, unbroken slope of granite so steep as to be entirely inaccessible to man. Pike's, Gray's, Long's and the host of other Rocky Mountain summits are tame when compared with the Grand Teton, and, viewed in the light of difficult and dangerous climbing, are not to be spoken in the same breath with it. It is absolutely peerless.

To attempt an ascent of this mighty peak, Mr. Dawson and myself, accompanied by our wives, proceeded to Market Lake, Idaho from which point the journey was completed by wagon, packs, and foot, the last eight miles being impassable by either of the former two methods. Market Lake, the nearest railway point to the Three Tetons, lies a hundred miles west of the peaks, and from this point these giant landmarks seemed to pierce the sky in their awful reach heavenward. At Basin River Ranch, thirty miles from the Teton Range, we secured an excellent photograph of the three peaks bathed in brilliant sunlight and carved on a band of bluest heaven. They looked bare and inaccessible. Proceeding eastward we reached our last camp on the Teton River, eight miles from the peaks and at once began preparation to "foot it" the remaining distance, wagons or packs from this point forward being out of the question. Taking a limited supply of bacon, flour, coffee, and sugar and barometer, thermometer, and camera, we set out the following morning accompanied by Alonzo Daw, our guide. Bedding was, or course, entirely out of the question.

At four o'clock in the afternoon, after a day of frightful climbing, we found ourselves on the west brink of the Teton cañon, a wild gorge of appalling depth and awful grandeur. From our feet a slope of forty-five degrees over beds of bowlders and ancient glacial moraines fell swiftly away to a snow-fed river at the bottom of the cañon three thousand feet distant.

We camped on the brink of the river, in a grassy plot amid a cluster of firs, at an altitude of 9,200 feet, and proceeded at once with the preparation of our evening meal. The women were in

Billy Owen's photograph of the Cathedral Group proves that the climber and surveyor was an accomplished photographer as well. *American Heritage Center, University of Wyoming*

the best of spirits, and had borne up under the fatiguing tramp with heroic fortitude, and were now eager to begin the ascent.

Our camp at this point was extremely picturesque, pitched as it was amid solemn pines, the sombre cañon walls rising hundreds of feet on either side, and broidered at the brink with mammoth banks of snow, affording the birthplace for a hundred cascades that leaped noisily over cold vertical walls of naked granite a thousand feet high.

Supper over, a bed of pine boughs under shelter of a huge log was arranged, and a large pile of wood collected with which to replenish the fire during the night. Having no bedding, it was necessary to keep up a good fire throughout the night. We retire—if I may use the expression—at dark, with nothing save the star-studded firmament for a covering, and as I lay there in the awful depths of that cañon mentally weighing the chances of sucess or failure for the morrow, the full moon rose tranquilly over the granite battlements of the Three Tetons, completely filling the cañon with its mellow light, and touching with a hand of gold the snow-capped pinnacles that stood like sentinels on the brink of the gorge.

I have never seen a more glorious exhibition of nature's wild beauty than here lay before me. There may be steeper cañons than this, and perhaps more beautiful, but there are none wider nor more rugged; and save for the golden sheen of the world-renowned Yellowstone cañon were difficult indeed to choose between them. After a hasty breakfast, provided with coils of rope, barometer, and thermometer, we crossed the snowy river and began the ascent of the steep comb or ridge that lay to the east, completely shutting the peaks from view. Two hours of painful climbing over beds of loose rock that were ready to start at any moment brought us to the crest of the ridge, no wider than a horse's back, and which, sweeping in a semi-circle to the south, joins the main range at the south side of the middle Teton. Looking eastward through a mile of superlatively clear atmosphere, we beheld the Grand Teton, unveiled from foot to crown—a giant monolith rising a clear 5,000 feet from the glacier valley at its base, and terminating in a point as sharp as the steeple of a church.

Words cannot convey the impression one gets while viewing that awful spire from this point. Its size and appalling height are simply overwhelming. In an experience of fifteen years of mountaineering I have seen absolutely nothing comparable with it. Five thousand feet of naked, cold granite, with not a spear of vegetation nor vestige of soil on the whole mountain. Sky, snow, and granite the only elements in this wild picture!

Descending gently, we encountered the west edge of a glacier lying peacefully in the amphitheater-like valley, resembling in contour the half of an oyster-shell with its small point broken off. It is nearly a mile wide, almost the same in length and has a maximum depth estimated at two hundred feet. The rope, to guard against accidents, was now put to use, but the glacier, having a gentle slope, and no crevasses to speak of, was crossed without difficulty. We were now at the actual foot of the peak and the ascent began, our path proceeding over a mass of loose rock, to scale which entailed the greatest danger to life and limb. At times large bowlders, becoming detached, would rush down the steep slope with irresistible velocity, filling the valley with echoes and threatening to carry the entire mass of loose rock to the bottom.

A thousand feet from the base, resort to the rope became necessary, and for the remainder of the distance scarcely a foot's progress could be made without it. Crevasses forty or fifty feet wide, filled with deep blue ice, were frequently encountered, constituting obstacles of a most dangerous character, and which, without the rope, would have been simply impassable.

Up, up, over nearly vertical walls of snow and ice-robed granite we toiled, reaching, after a desperate struggle, an altitude of 13,200 feet, at a point on the south side of the peak.

Here, toward the east, the face of the mountain sweeps down in a long, unbroken slope of glacier-polished rock for six thousand feet, meeting at the base a score of Alpine lakes fringed with lofty pines. And at this point defeat stared us in the face at every turn. A thousand feet above our heads towered bare, rocky pinnacles without crack or crevice to afford hold for foot or hand, and as vertical as a plumb-line. It might be possible to make the ascent from the north side, but we had no time to reconnoitre, for it was already three o'clock and camp was a good distance off. We were completely baffled, and none felt the disappointment so keenly as the women, whose skill and courage thus far had been little short of marvelous.

A hundred miles to the southeast, shimmering in the blue, stood Fremont's Peak, conspicuous among a host of others whose giant forms stood in faultless definition.

Being unable to continue the ascent, we chiseled our names on the rock, and erected a large cairn in which we deposited an air-tight can containing the date and brief account of our trip and an excellent portrait of our Secretary of State, Mr. James G. Blaine. It had been our intention from the beginning, if we reached the summit, to christen this peerless peak in honor of our great statesman, as being the only mountain in our country worthy to bear his name.

Beginning the descent, we were soon enveloped in a blinding snow storm with ragged flashes of lightning and terrific peals of thunder, whose vibrations detached large blocks of stone that came thundering down the mountain side with the velocity of a bullet. I had often read in Whymper's "Scrambles Among the Alps," of cannonades on the Matterhorn, but never realized before now the terror that such an exhibition can inspire. The snow, completely wetting the rock, rendered the descent far more dangerous than the climb had been, and compelled the use of the rope continually. However, we reached the glacier in safety, which terminated the more difficult portion of the descent, and proceeded to cross the field of snow, which had become, during our absence, literally covered with blocks of stone, rolled hither by the jar consequent of the heavy thunder accompanying the storm. Without an accident we reached camp at seven o'clock thoroughly drenched and cold, and considerably cast down by our failure to reach the summit. A large fire, however, soon dispelled the gloom, and served in a great measure to restore our spirits.

Whether the Teton be inaccessible or not, I am not quite prepared to say. It is no mountain for novice, however, for failure certainly awaits any but the most skillful, and even such a one will require every appliance known to the fraternity to overcome the obstacles which beset him on this grandest peak of the Rocky Mountains. There are many peaks in the Rockies as lofty as the Teton, but beyond this point all parallelism ceases.

The country surrounding the peaks is rugged and wild beyond the power of words to convey, and when this region becomes more accessible, by means of railroads already projected, it will doubtless rival, as a pleasuring ground, the famous National Park itself.

The scenery of the whole Teton country is intensely interesting. Its sombre forests, opening gradually upward and terminating in scattered groves of individual beauty; its deep and rugged

A diminutive Owen celebrates the naming of Mt. Owen with Ranger Fritiof Fryxell and an unidentified companion. *American Heritage Center, University of Wyoming*

cañons with massive, precipitous walls; its turbulent and varied cascades; its extensive snow fields with broad patches of virgin white gracefully trimming the lofty, needle-like summits, together form a combination of grandeur and beauty which may not be described.

And then, in addition to all this, stands that awful spire of granite whose storm-swept summit knows not the foot of man— a naked column of rock rising abruptly seven thousand feet from the valley and terminating in a point sharp as the spike of a warrior's helmet. However exalted may be the expectation, none can behold and be disappointed. It is a peak in every way worthy the attempt of that veteran mountaineer, Mr. Edward Whymper, and wears with distinguished honor the second title we gave it—the Matterhorn of America.

PART TWO

HUNTING FOR BIG GAME

Owen Wister
Great God! I've Just
Killed a Bear

Owen Wister needs little introduction in Wyoming or the West. He is the author of The Virginian *(1900), a novel of cattlemen, cowboys, rustling, and romance set in the background of the vast mountains and grasslands of Wyoming. The book is considered the prototype of hundreds of western books and films to follow.*

It is not well known that Wister familiarized himself with Wyoming long before he sat down to write his classic novel. The well-heeled Philadel-phian first came in 1885, following his graduation from Harvard. Each succeeding year the drudgery of law school was followed by an exhilarating summer in Wyoming where Wister gathered adventures and ideas.

The following selections include a brief note from his 1887 diary regarding a bear, and a lengthier one the following year. The latter rather humorously chronicles his adventures in finding Leigh and Jenny Lakes, and then hunting, fishing, and climbing nearby.

Saturday, August 13. Great God! I've just killed a bear, and I'm writing this by his bloody carcass—6:30 A.M.

I looked down towards Jackson Hole and saw the ragged leavings of the thunder cloud prowling up the slopes of pine hills, beyond which the ice-sharp points of the Tetons glittered with snow and sunlight, and over the basin hung a brilliant golden cloud that swam in the rays, while all the other clouds were black or gray.

As I write [in the evening after killing the bear], we hear the ominous howl of some beast that would like to come into camp, and may before morning. The Ward-Dimmick hunting party that started from Washakie after us came and camped next door this evening. But they realize they are trespassing on our hunting field and are to move on tomorrow. Also there is a horse thief hanging about them and us. Altogether we are in good company with the bears, the catamount now howling, and the horse thief lurking about in an unoccupied manner. He sat by our fire tonight for about an hour without speaking a sentence or meeting anyone's eye. How we killed the bear I must record tomorrow, as it is ten (very late), and George and I get up at four to visit the bait. It is fearfully cold.

Tuesday, August 16, 8:30 P.M. I return to Saturday's work. We went to bed Friday night, having settled that George and I with Tigie should visit the south bait in the morning. The weather was uncertain. Sometime during the night I waked and heard rain patting the canvas overhead steadily. Later I waked again in the dull gray and shivered and was sorry we were going to any bait at five in the morning. I went to sleep, hoping Tigie and West (who was to wake us and give us something to eat) would oversleep. But they didn't. My foot was pulled, and I rose and shivered into my cold greasy boots. We had some tea and bread and started.

The way was uphill at once, and in this altitude (the aneroid registers 8900 with a fall in the weather that probably would take 600 off the reading of the barometer) breathing is a desultory operation, and a rifle becomes wonderfully heavy in five minutes. But it was necessary to follow Tigie like his shadow. I tried to make as little noise as he did, slipping by jagged rotten boughs, letting his shoulder go an inch from them and stepping over the twigs that lay thick in the timber. His moccasins slipped over them with never a crack. Luckily the rain had wet the ground enough for the twigs to be pliant; so our boots made much less noise than they would after a dry night.

And so we went over the grass and under the trees till we came to a gulch where a little stream flowed, and Tigie pointed among the trees where the bait was, though it was too far among the thickets to see. We became more silent and snaky as we circled beyond the place to come down on it under cover. Just then the sun rose feebly into a very light blue sky and sent some useless rays across the tops of the pine trees behind us. Now we peered over some brushwood at the bait. It hung there alone, and as we searched its neighborhood a squirrel burst into scolding directly beside us. After the sudden start it gave me, coming in the middle of such a tense silence, I could have flayed that squirrel alive. He would have suggested danger to any moderately intelligent bear. Also some of the gray carrion crow birds that swarm in this country began to talk and caw. So we came up close to the bait and saw it had been torn and mangled by big jaws recently. The other piece near it, but just inside the timber, was untouched. Tigies said that at sunset the bear would return and so should we. We returned our steps somewhat wearily and found breakfast hot.

As we were finishing it, Tigie, who had gone to get the horses into camp, suddenly appeared over the rise to the northeast of camp beckoning violently from his horse. I grabbed my rifle and rushed across our bathroom and pantry (viz., a stoney little hole in the thread of water on which we are camped) and up through the wet brush to him. "Bear! Bear!" he said. "Jump up here. Go. Quick." He had seen a bear crossing on the edge of the timber some three hundred yeards beyond. So I jumped on the bare rump of his horse and sat there behind Tigie, my rifle in one hand, the other on his shoulder. Away he started, trotting and galloping. My horror was that I should slide off somewhere with a crash and ruin the whole thing. For the way we went was over anything that happened to be in the straight line that Tigie made for the gulch that we had lately left. Down across the stones of dry water channels, up their banks perpendicularly, under limbs of trees bending right and left to avoid them. I have never taken such a ride. Then we came across the gulch a good deal above the bait, and the feeling of hush came down hard on me.

As a freshman at Harvard, Owen Wister participated in theater. However, he much preferred his summer adventures in the American West. *American Heritage Center, University of Wyoming*

Tigie whispered, "Over there, way over, down." I saw nothing but a wide grass clearing and pines beyond, but I got down among the sparse trees and so did Tigie. Then we crept forward. Tigie put me up front, and as I looked over my shoulder at him for directions I caught the horse's eye as he found himself alone, left behind watching after us with anxious self-control.

Then again Tigie said, "There," and crouched against the grass.

I looked across some three hundred yards to the edge of the pines and saw the bear leisurely sauntering along. I had wondered how it would be with me when this moment should come, and now found myself simply submerged in staring—no excitement, at best no shaking of any nerves, but only my eyes misted on that big beast as he rolled along by the edge of the wood. He looked brown and gray, and his gestures were those of a good-natured old gentleman taking a little morning air for health's sake. Now he would wag his head, then gaze at the landscape judicially, then pause at a rotten trunk on the ground, or sit up with it between his paws looking for insects on the damp underside.

"Quick," said Tigie behind me. "He comes then—so-so," pointing the course the bear would come along.

I hurried forward nearly parallel to the bear's march and sat behind a good wide tree, Tigie at my side. The sun was now bright as I looked across the intervening grass. The bear arrived at where the line of woodland curved down more in my direction, rounding off the end of the lawn some hundred yards ahead of where I sat holding my rifle and wondering when it would begin to be unsteady in my grip. Slowly the bear came down, admiring the weather and pulling his rotten logs. Then he passed behind a tree that stood in the middle of the open. I looked at Tigie, who nodded. Then I ran forward out on the grass, and the bear's head came out from the further side of my tree. I shifted my course so that he and I were like the opposite spokes of a wheel of which the tree was the center, only I neared the tree as quickly as I could. Each time the bear's snout showed to the right of it, I edged to the left correspondingly. When I got under its branches, I stood up full height (for I had been mincing along in a very hunched up position), and the bear walked out into full view on the other side. He saw me and stopped short. Well, my hand's steady after all, I said to myself, as I looked at him along my rifle barrel. I remembered how the brown hair on his shoulder looked thick. I heard my rifle crack and saw him fall at once on his head with a slanting kind of rush and near enough for me to see the dirt scatter a little from his claws.

"Shoot, shoot!" screamed Tigie from behind. I did as I was bid, but I was loath to do it—that first lucky shot had been enough. He tried to get up twice, and before he was half way up his feet they rolled up under him and he tumbled in a heap each time, head downwards. But I shot.

"Shoot! shoot!" said Tigie, running out from his tree, and he worked his arms as if he held the lever of the Winchester himself. I felt like a murderer as I pumped the bullets into the poor old gentleman who swayed about on the grass, utterly gone. My last shot went through part of the skull and down into his throat almost to the shoulder, where I afterwards found its flattened remains. We turned him over and rode back to camp, where I found the betting was three to one against my having hit anything.

• • • • • •

Here begins Western trip the third—may I someday write the thirtieth with as much zest! We have been going most of two days now. Yesterday morning, George Norman and Bob Simes met each other at Jersey City and met me at Philadelphia.

Sunday Morning, July 29, 1888, Headwaters of Wind River. We came here up the narrowing valley, past old man Clark and his domicile, the last inhabitant we shall see. Bobby missed an antelope. I missed a big gander with my rifle, but luckily Paul and George got the young ones by chasing them. They were very good at supper. Here Wind River leads up into the timber and is gone. This meadow is the last one. Ahead of us the woods close in.

Above to the right is a glorious fortress of rock half a mile long—hundreds of feet above the highest timber—and broken into battlements and turrets by the hundred, with a big stone man sitting at one end watching the valley. The sun shines along this whole line, leaving the crevices filled with a pale blue floating colour while the buttresses stand out brown-yellow in the daylight. There's another fortress to the left and a long regular line of wall joining the two, with a green timbered hill rising in front of it—and so Wind River begins its journey.

Wednesday Afternoon, August 8. This camp we came to on Sunday, and we had to work to get here. First I will correct a slight error. Our last camp on the Snake just below Crawford's shack was not six miles away from the Tetons but fifteen at least, as every one of this party can now testify through painful experience. The atmosphere in this country is like all other mountain atmosphere—tricky. After a sharp rain last Saturday evening, Bobby and I set out for the geese which Paul had seen in a slue of the river just above. It was too late. Moreover, had we shot any, a boat would have been necessary to get at them, for a large belt of willow swamp makes approach to their feeding ground impossible. But what was tantalizing was the sight of five sand-hill crane roosting on one leg along a sand island, hopelessly out of reach. I never eat a bird I thought better than the sand-hill crane we had on the Snake a year ago. May have been self and stomach, but think it was the bird. Bobby and I returned to camp, drenched through with the marsh, and found George had caught some dubious looking fish, whose taste at breakfast was more dubious still.

On Sunday morning George and I consulted the maps and found out just where we wished to go and just where we are now camped—but no thanks to the natives for that. The trouble that morning was twofold; Paul LeRose was having an old man's fit of crustiness (owing to his insides, I think), and he had never been or heard of where we wanted to go. He told us in husky and forbidding tones that he did not know the country west of the Snake. When we made a diffident allusion to two lakes that lay south of Jackson Lake, under the Tetons (we did not dare to call them their United States map Christian names, since the bare idea of a map gives Paul acute nervous trouble), Paul said he had never heard that there were any lakes there. This was his method of denying their existence. Then, how to cross the Snake at this place? Well, we told him to go and find a crossing at once, and in the meantime George and I went up a hill to survey our route but learned nothing in particular except that the prickly pear will penetrate a moccasin. After a while we packed and got away, a crossing of course being found within a mile.

Monday, August 13. Why all the horses did not break each a leg or two, I cannot explain. I never was in a worse place. Long wet grass and weeds completely hid the scaffolding of rotting and rotten pine trunks that lay across this piece of marsh, and the ground was so boggy that often your horse lurched up to his shoulders in it and the frantically plunged forward and fell against the hidden timber. At the edge of this where trees began and the land suddenly rose steep, we became securely netted. Spikey trunks pointed down the hill, and had to be jumped over from loose stones to loose stones. Any pack horse with pretence to originality of mind chose a separate trail for himself and after following it a while, halted at a good distance off from the rest of us. My horse nearly fell backwards with me, so I hurried off of him into the oozy patch of mud. Getting over this piece of our road (certainly our road, for nobody ever used it before, and nobody will ever use it again) took an hour, and it was not much more than three hundred yards we traveled from the beginning of the swamp to clear going. There we followed up the Snake River, which flows nearly due east here before bending south to Buffalo Fork. Presently it spread into the beginning of Jackson Lake, and still we kept along shore.

The lakes we were aiming for, we were pretty sure, lay south of our direction to some degree anyhow, but Paul, the crusty, continued his way in the van. I spoke to George, but George said we were going properly, and to a certain extent he was right. We were aiming generally for anywhere along the two little lakes west of the river, and had we continued as we were going, we should finally have come out (or rather scraped under and

Owen Wister and friends roughing it in the West. Wister is standing, pouring a drink from a flask for his Indian guide, Tigie. *American Heritage Center, University of Wyoming*

climbed through) on the northeast shore of the north lake. That route would have increased our experience of timber if we have not already enough for a liberal Wyoming education.

I gradually grew nearly as crusty as Paul—and kept riding to the south of the outfit, which Paul observed clearly enough but never turned a hair. At last we came to a fork and turned southwest, after having gone round two bays the lake made, instead of cutting south of them and so saving time, trouble, and temper. Dick Washakie's derision of Old Paul waked up now, for he said, "What a ridiculous trail we are taking." Dick, whole breed of Indian, has continual amusement out of Paul, half-breed and white man, as near as he can do it. Paul declines to speak anything but English to the Indians and affects to be without their instinct for trail-finding. But he claims a special white gift of his own for that Art. So Paul took us south, but not enough, and always into needless and very vile timber. So we came to the fork again and told him to keep out of the timber in the sagebursh, and he did.

All this time the great Teton range had declined to come nearer though we had been making for it since starting. At length we did make some impression on distance, for when you looked up the valleys between the peaks, you could distinguish particular trees from the mass and see the water moving down. Paul had now got to riding about due south, though we had pointed out to him a sinking of the pine woods, just at the foot of the two most southern mountains, which held out promises of a lake or of water at any rate.

As we passed a thinner share in the timber to our right which looked as if it might get us near the mountains pretty clear of tree-trunks, I suggested going through that way to George, who agreed. Paul ventilated some wrath. "Why did you tell me to keep out of timber if you want to go right among it?" I diffidently said that I thought it looked thinner—and then added that of course I didn't know the ways of the country very well and if he thought that would take us into bad timber, we'd not go. "No, you chose that way and you shall go," snarled ancient Paul, and in we went. Then I think he thought he'd box me up—for he said, "I don't know which way you want to go. You ride in front now." So I did, and very fortunately I had hit on a pretty good pass between thick woods—and we all got through without entanglement. George's horse cut up—dashed him against a tree and banged his jaw—but nothing really serious. I steered as well as I could for the dip in the woods below the range, and we came out on a big sage park. Paul has ceased to be crusty and rode alongside talking affably on many topics. Then I rode ahead some way to a ridge to look over if possible, but woods stood in the way. It had been very hot for many hours, and nobody had had any water or food.

As I stood on the ridge, I heard far off coming from the dip a faint and sustained roar. When Paul came up, I made him listen. He said it sounded like water, and we went on. He had been very sceptical about lakes and water over here all day, and presently it returned to him. We went up a ridge over which we expected to find ourselves close to mountains and water, and then in front stretched a big yellow waste of sage and cobble stones as wide and flat and dry as the ones we had just crossed. On the farther side of it a belt of pines, and then the mountains rose at once.

"Well, we shall see camp without water tonight," said Paul with a cackle of triumph, though not a joyful one.

"Listen again," I said. The roar was just as sustained as before and much louder.

"Oh, that's the mountain wind," said Paul.

Then Bobby came by and said that George said the lakes must be east of us now—there could be no room for them in front. Till this I had kept unshaken faith in lakes and water ahead, but now I passed a bad quarter of an hour during which Dick came by hilariously repeating, "No water! Camp tonight—no water!" and West looked at the belt of pines and saw no cottonwood, which led him to join the chorus.

But where, I thought, in creation is a big mountain range 20 miles long and 13,000 feet high with snow in giant patches and green valleys and no water at all at the bottom? Possible in the moon—but on this planet, nowhere. The situation grew strained, for we seemed now about two hundred yards [from] the rise of the Tetons. Dick rode ahead and came back laughing. "All right," he said. And so we came to a big rushing stream which slipped out of a placid shallow spread above and went into the woods below, foaming down rocks, perfectly clear and not cold. Next day we found one lake ten minutes ride above us and the other lake fifteen minutes walk below us, and water enough to drown yourself in or to float a fleet in—of canoes anyhow. The lake below us is the best of the two—very deep and jammed with trout. I'll detail here the resources of this camp. Of the following fauna and flora all have been killed, seen, or eaten by one of the party: black currants, raspberries, strawberries, red and blue huckleberries (the red new to me, and very sweet) trout, duck, mink, otter, porcupine, beaver, fox, antelope, blacktail deer, elk, moose, and an unknown black quadruped seen by Bobby and not likely to be anybody's dog.

Our camp could hardly be better, and we struck exactly the best place along this water system—below and above us is too much timber and too little pasture. On Monday, winning the matching, I hunted with Paul north—in timber all the time. Late in the day had a good shot at an elk and hit him. He fell down and kicked, and so like a fool when he got up and stood vaguely looking about, I concluded one shot enough and did not fire again. He had not fallen at once but sank down slowly. Well, he got away, and Paul was justly enraged. So was I, but luckily he and Dick found him an hour or so later, and we eat him. I should have probably found him myself; but Paul was so disgusted that with that and his affectation of not being an Indian he lost the elk's trail and got us all snarled up away off—and so we came home.

I don't yet claim to have the hunting training enough to follow a trail with unless there's more blood than this bore—but my economy of shots on this occasion was the act of a chump. Bobby went out with Dick, and maybe he saw a moose. Paul saw one with me, but the moose had the wind of us and left the country.

Next day, Tuesday, Bobby went with Paul, George with Dick. The latter saw not even a fresh track (to the south). Bobby unluckily missed about five animals, including all the venison species in the neighborhood. West and I struggled up the mountain range and found a lake perched about three hundred feet above us and game trail so thick that in spots it smelt like cow stables. Sounds Western and romantic this—but quite true. We also found the mountain as mountains usually are, higher than when seen from the bottom. Going up took us four hours. Very steep all the way—first grass, then rocks, and lastly snow and shale. We did not get to any peak but up to a collar between over which we could look into a wild country below—and blue mountains far beyond in Idaho. The view of the basin on this side has given me a permanent and very accurate idea of the whole country here. On the way down we saw two otter. Next day our account of this ascent sent George, Bobby, and Dick up. They took much longer—having all day—and reached West and myself and afternoon tea on the lake up the hill. Next day, Thursday, we concentrated forces on young trout and netted some two hundred—making a whitebait effect of them that was quite taking. I sat with my legs bare in the water on logs too long in the morning and therefore suffered horribly from sunburn. Fishing for big trout in the afternoon I fell in to my waist and neglected to do anything about it. So got slowly and surely chilled and then sick.

On Saturday, I went off alone to see if any trail could be found over into Idaho between the Grand Teton and the next to the north, opposite which we are. But one way round the lake I did nothing but empale my poor horse in the timber, luckily not deep, and the other way round I found also impracticable by reason of timber into which I did not penetrate. On this ride I spent a long time crawling over the baking cobble stones and trying to screen my carcass from three antelope behind sultry clumps of sagebrush. The antelope grazed on, suspicious but not alarmed, and slowly grazed their way to a position where nothing but pancake could have approached them unobserved. So I gave up and came into camp weary and my sickness not gone but worse apparently. This day two mink came tearing into camp together, all among the pots and kettles while all but I were at dinner. They were proposing marriage on the spot—and therefore ignored all other things. Result—she escaped, his skin hangs on a tree. Paul has trapped a fine beaver.

Theodore Roosevelt
An Elk-Hunt
at Two-Ocean Pass

Theodore Roosevelt's conservation accomplishments are legendary. He established six times more national forests than any other president. He signed national parks bills into law and made liberal use of the Antiquities Act of 1906 to establish national monuments. Almost all of these land withdrawals were in the American West. Those who use and appreciate the public lands and parks owe Roosevelt much for his wise stewardship.

Unlike Chester Arthur, President Roosevelt was intimately acquainted with the West. He wrote its history, Winning of the West, *in four volumes, and owned a ranch in the Badlands of North Dakota. Above all, he hunted big game throughout the mountains and plains. Almost a compulsive writer, he often wrote of his adventures for the more prestigious magazines of his day, such as* Scribner's *or* Century Magazine. *The following is an 1892 account of a hunting expedition in the Teton Wilderness area, then known as the Thoroughfare region, comprising the Continental Divide, and separating Jackson Hole from Yellowstone and the Atlantic drainage from that of the Pacific. Today it is an officially-designated wilderness area and is still famed for its beauty and superb hunting.*

ONE FALL with my ranch-partner Ferguson, I made an elk-hunt in northwestern Wyoming among the Shoshone Mountains, where they join the Hoodoo and Absoraka ranges. There is no more beautiful game-country in the United States. It is a park-land, where glades, meadows, and high mountain pastures break the evergreen forest: a forest which is open compared to the tangled density of the woodland farther north. It is a high, cold region of many lakes and clear, rushing streams. The steep mountains are generally of the rounded form so often seen in the ranges of the Cordilleras of the United States; but the Hoodoos, or Goblins, are carved in fantastic and extraordinary shapes; while the Tetons, a group of isolated rock peaks, show a striking boldness in their lofty outlines.

This was one of the pleasantest hunts I ever made. As always in the mountains, save where the country is so rough and so densely wooded that one must go afoot, we had a pack-train; and we took a more complete outfit than we had ever before taken on such a hunt, and so traveled in much comfort. Usually, when in the mountains, I have merely had one companion, or at most two, and two or three pack-ponies; each of us doing his share of the packing, cooking, fetching water, and pitching the small square of canvas which served as tent. In itself packing is both an art and a mystery, and a skillful professional packer, versed in the intricacies of the "diamond hitch," packs with a speed which no non-professional can hope to rival, and fixes the side packs and top packs with such scientific nicety, and adjusts the doubles and turns of the lashrope so accurately, that every-thing stays in place under any but the most adverse conditions. Of course, like most hunters, I myself can in case of need throw the diamond hitch, after a fashion, and pack on either the off or near side. Indeed, unless a man can pack, it is not possible to make a really hard hunt in the mountains, if alone, or with only a single companion.

On this trip we had with us two hunters, Tazewell Woody and Elwood Hofer, a packer who acted as cook, and a boy to herd the horses. Of the latter there were twenty; six saddle-animals and fourteen for the packs, two or three being spare horses, to be used later in carrying the elk-antlers, sheep-horns, and other trophies. Like most hunters' pack-animals, they were

A well-outfitted hunting party about to depart from Jackson. Such men as Stephen Leek, Ben Sheffield and others made their living from Jackson Hole's fame as a hunting mecca. *American Heritage Center, University of Wyoming*

either half broken, or else broken down; tough, unkempt, jaded-looking beasts of every color—sorrel, buckskin, pinto, white, bay, roan. After the day's work was over, they were turned loose to shift for themselves; and about once a week they strayed and all hands had to spend the better part of the day hunting for them. The worst ones for straying, curiously enough, were three broken-down old "bear-baits," which went by themselves, as is generally the case with the cast-off horses of a herd. There were two sleeping-tents, another for the provisions,—in which we ate during bad weather,— and a canvas teepee, which was put up with lodge-poles, Indian fashion, like a wigwam. A teepee is more difficult to put up than an ordinary tent; but it is very convenient when there is rain or snow. A small fire kindled in the middle keeps it warm, the smoke escaping through the open top; that is, when it escapes at all. Strings are passed from one pole to another, on which to hang wet clothes and shoes, and the beds are made round the edges. As an offset to the warmth and shelter, the smoke often renders it impossible even to sit upright. We had a very good camp-kit, including plenty of cooking- and eating-utensils; and among our provisions were some canned goods and sweetmeats, to give a relish to our meals of meat and bread. We had fur coats and warm clothes, which are chiefly needed at night, and plenty of bedding, including water-proof canvas sheeting and two caribou-hide sleeping-bags, procured from the survivors of a party of arctic explorers. Except on rainy days I used my buckskin hunting-shirt or tunic; in dry weather I deem it, because of its color, texture, and durability, the best possible garb for the still-hunter, especially in the woods.

Starting a day's journey south of Heart Lake, we traveled and hunted on the eastern edge of the great basin, wooded and mountainous, wherein rise the head waters of the mighty Snake River. There was not so much as a spotted line,—that series of blazes made with the ax, man's first highway through the hoary forest,—but this we did not mind, as for most of the distance we followed well-worn elk trails. The train traveled in Indian file. At the head, to pick the path, rode tall, silent old Woody, a true type of the fast-vanishing race of game-hunters and Indian-fighters, a man who had been once of the California forty-niners, and who ever since had lived the restless, reckless life of the wilderness. Then came Ferguson and I; then the pack-animals, strung out in line; while from the rear rose the varied oaths of our three companions, whose miserable duty it was to urge forward the beasts of burden.

It is heart-breaking work to drive a pack-train through thick timber and over mountains, where there is either a dim trail or none. The animals have a perverse faculty for choosing the wrong turn at critical moments, and they are continually scraping under branches and squeezing between tree-trunks, to the jeopardy or destruction of the burdens. After having been laboriously driven up a very steep incline, at the cost of severe exertion both to them and to the men, the foolish creatures turn and run down to the bottom, so that all the work has to be done over again. Some travel too slow, others travel too fast; yet one cannot but admire the toughness of the animals, and the sure-footedness with which they pick their way along the sheer mountain-sides, or among boulders and over fallen logs.

As our way was so rough, we found that we had to halt at least once every hour to fix the packs. Moreover, we at the head of the column were continually being appealed to for help by the unfortunates in the rear. First it would be "that white-eyed cayuse; one side of its pack's down!" then we would be notified that the saddle-blanket of the "lop-eared Indian buckskin" had slipped back; then a shout "Look out for the pinto!" would be followed by that pleasing beast's appearance, bucking and squealing, smashing dead timber, and scattering its load to the four winds. It was no easy task to get the horses across some of the boggy places without miring, or to force them through the denser portions of the forest, where there was much down timber. Riding with a pack-train, day in and day out, becomes both monotonous and irritating, unless one is upheld by the hope of a game-country ahead, or by the delight of exploration of the unknown. Yet when buoyed by such a hope, there is pleasure in taking a train across so beautiful and wild a country as that which lay on the threshold of our hunting-grounds in the Sho-shones. We went over mountain passes, with ranges of scalped peaks on each hand; we skirted the edges of lovely lakes, and of streams with boulder-strewn beds; we plunged into depths of somber woodland, broken by wet prairies. It was a picturesque sight to see the loaded pack-train stringing across one of these high mountain meadows, the motley-colored line of ponies winding round the marshy spots through the bright green grass, while beyond rose the dark line of frowning forest, with lofty peaks towering in the background. Some of the meadows were beautiful with many flowers—goldenrod, purple aster, blue-bells, white immortelles, and here and there masses of blood-red Indian pinks. In the park-country, on the edges of the evergreen forest, were groves of delicate quaking-aspen, the trees often growing to a considerable height; their tremulous leaves were already changing to bright green and yellow, occasionally with a reddish blush. In the Rocky Mountains the aspens are almost the only deciduous trees, their foliage offering a pleasant relief to the eye after the monotony of the unending pine and spruce woods, which afford so striking a contrast to the hard-wood forest east of the Mississippi.

For two days our journey was uneventful, save that we came on the camp of a squaw-man, one Beaver Dick, an old mountain hunter, living in a skin tepee, where dwelt his comely Indian wife and half-breed children. He had quite a herd of horses, many of them mares and colts; they had evidently been well treated, and came up to us fearlessly.

The morning of the third day of our journey was gray and lowering. Gusts of rain blew in my face as I rode at the head of the train. It still lacked an hour of noon, as we were plodding up a valley, beside a rapid brook running through narrow willow-flats, with the dark forest crowding down on each hand from the low foot-hills of the mountains. Suddenly the call of a bull elk came echoing down through the wet woodland on our right, beyond the brook, seemingly less than half a mile off, and was answered by a faint, far-off call from a rival on the mountain beyond. Instantly halting the train, Woody and I slipped off, our horses, crossed the brook, and started to still-hunt for the first bull.

In this place the forest was composed of western tamarack; the large, tall tress stood well apart, and there was much down timber, but the ground was covered with deep, wet moss, over which we trod silently. The elk was traveling up-wind, but slowly, stopping continually to paw the ground and to thrash the bushes with his antlers. He was very noisy, challenging every minute or two, being doubtless much excited by the neighbor-hood of his rival on the mountain. We followed, Woody leading, guided by the incessant calling.

It was very exciting as we crept toward the great bull, and the challenge sounded nearer and nearer. While we were still at some distance the pealing notes were like those of a bugle, delivered in two bars, first rising, then abruptly falling; as we drew nearer they took on a harsh, squealing sound. Each call made our veins thrill; it sounded like the cry of some huge beast of prey. At last we heard the roar of the challenge not eighty yards off. Stealing forward three or four rods, I saw the tips of the horns through a mass of dead timber and young growth, and slipped to one side to get a clean shot. Seeing us, but not making out what we were, and full of fierce and insolent excitement, the wapiti bull stepped boldly toward us with a stately, swinging gait. Then he stood motionless, facing us, barely fifty yards away, his handsome twelve-tined antlers tossed aloft, as he held his head with the lordly grace of his kind. I fired into his chest, and as he turned I raced forward and shot him in the flank; but the second bullet was not needed, for the first wound was mortal, and he fell before going fifty yards.

The dead elk lay among the young evergreens. The huge, shapely body was set on legs that were as strong as steel rods, and yet slender, clean, and smooth; they were in color a beautiful dark brown, contrasting well with the yellowish of the body. The neck and throat were garnished with a mane of long hair; the symmetry of the great horns set off the fine, delicate lines of the noble head. He had been wallowing, as elk are fond of doing, and the dried mud clung in patches to his flank; a stab in the haunch showed that he had been overcome in battle by some master bull, who had turned him out of the herd.

We cut off the head, and bore it down to the train. The horses crowded together, snorting, with their ears pricked forward, as they smelled the blood. We also took the loins with us, as we were out of meat, though bull elk in the rutting season is not very good. The rain had changed to a steady downpour when we again got under way. Two or three miles further we pitched camp in a clump of pines on a hillock in the bottom of the valley, starting hot fires of pitchy stumps before the tents, to dry our wet things.

Next day opened with fog and cold rain. The drenched pack-animals, when driven into camp, stood mopingly, with drooping heads and arched backs; they groaned and grunted as the loads were placed on their backs and the cinches tightened, the packers bracing one foot against the pack to get a purchase as they hauled in on the lash-rope. A stormy morning is a trial to temper: the packs are wet and heavy, and the cold makes the work even more than usually hard on the hands. By ten we broke camp. It needs between two and three hours to break camp and to get such a train properly packed; once started, our day's journey was from six to eight hours long, making no halt. We started up a steep, pine-clad mountainside, broken by cliffs. My hunting-shoes, though comfortable, were old and thin, and let the water through like a sieve. On the top of the first plateau, where black-spruce groves were strewn across the grassy surface, we saw a band of elk, cows and calves, trotting off through the rain. Then we plunged down into a deep valley, and, crossing it, a hard climb took us to the top of a great bare table-land, bleak and wind-swept. We passed little alpine lakes, fringed with scattering dwarf evergreens. Snow lay in drifts on the north sides of gullies; a cutting wind blew the icy rain in our faces. For two or three hours we traveled toward the farther edge of the table-land. In one place a spike-bull elk stood half a mile off in the open; he traveled to and fro, watching us.

As we neared the edge the storm lulled, and pale, watery sunshine gleamed through the rifts in the low-scudding clouds. At last our horses stood on the brink of a bold cliff. Deep down beneath our feet lay the wild and lonely valley of Two-Ocean Pass, walled in on each hand by rugged mountain-chains, their flanks scarred and gashed by precipice and chasm. Beyond, in a wilderness of jagged and barren peaks, stretched the Shoshones. At the middle point of the pass two streams welled down from each side. At first each flowed in but one bed, but soon divided into two; each of the twin branches then joined the like branch of the brook opposite, and swept one to the east and one to the west, on their long journey to the two great oceans. They ran as rapid brooks, through wet meadows and willow-flats, the eastern to the Yellowstone, the western to the Snake. The dark pine forests swept down from the flanks and lower ridges of the mountains to the edges of the marshy valley. Above them jutted gray rock peaks, snow-drifts lying in the rents that seamed their northern faces. Far below us, from a great basin at the foot of the cliff, filled with the pine forest, rose the musical challenge of

Although Theodore Roosevelt did not cross the sagebrush flats of Jackson Hole, his hunting company was similar to this party. *American Heritage Center, University of Wyoming*

a bull elk; and we saw a band of cows and calves looking like mice as they ran among the trees.

It was getting late, and after some search we failed to find any trail leading down; so at last we plunged over the brink at a venture. It was very rough scrambling, dropping from bench to bench, and in places it was not only difficult, but dangerous for the loaded pack-animals. Here and there we were helped by well-beaten elk-trails, which we could follow for several hundred yards at a time. On one narrow pine-clad ledge we met a spike-bull face to face, and in scrambling down a very steep, bare, rock-strewn shoulder the loose stones started by the horses' hoofs, bounding in great leaps to the forest below, dislodged two cows.

As evening fell, we reached the bottom, and pitched camp in a beautiful point of open pine forest thrust out into the meadow. There we found good shelter and plenty of wood, water, and grass; we built a huge fire and put up our tents, scattering them in likely places among the pines, which grew far apart and without undergrowth. We dried our steaming clothes, and ate a hearty supper of clk-meat; then we turned into our beds, warm and dry, and slept soundly under the canvas, while all night long the storm roared without.

Next morning dawned clear and cold, the sky a glorious blue. Woody and I started out to hunt over the great table-land, and led our stout horses up the mountain-side by elk-trails so bad that they had to climb like goats. All these elk-trails have one striking peculiarity: they lead through thick timber, but every now and then send off short, well-worn branches to some cliff-edge or jutting crag, commanding a view far and wide over the country beneath. Elk love to stand on these lookout points, and scan the valleys and mountains round about.

Blue grouse rose from beside our path; Clarke's crows flew past us, with a hollow, flapping sound, or lighted in the pine-tops, calling and flirting their tails; the gray-clad whisky-jacks, with multitudinous cries, hopped and fluttered near us. Snow-shoe rabbits scuttled away, the great furry feet which give them their name already turning white. At last we came out on the great plateau, seamed with deep, narrow ravines. Reaches of pasture alternated with groves and open forests of varying size. Almost immediately we heard the bugle of a bull elk, and saw a big band of cows and calves on the other side of the valley. There were three bulls with them, one very large, and we tried to creep up on them; but the wind was baffling, and spoiled our stalk. So we returned to our horses, mounted them, and rode a mile farther, toward a large open wood on a hillside. When within two hundred yards we heard directly ahead the bugle of a bull, and pulled up short. In a moment I saw him walking through an open glade; he had not seen us. The slight breeze brought us his scent. Elk have a strong characteristic smell; it is usually sweet, like that of a herd of Alderney cows, but in old bulls, while rutting, it is rank, pungent, and lasting. We stood motionless till the bull was out of sight, then stole to the wood, tied our horses, and trotted after him. He was traveling fast, occasionally calling, whereupon others in the neighborhood would answer. Evidently he had been driven out of some herd by the master bull.

He went faster than we did, and while we were vainly trying

to overtake him we heard another very loud and sonorous challenge to our left. It came from a ridge-crest at the edge of the woods, among some scattered clumps of the northern nut-pine, or piñon, a queer conifer, growing very high on the mountains, its multiforked trunk and wide-spreading branches giving it the rounded top and, at a distance, the general look of an oak rather than a pine. We at once walked toward the ridge, up-wind. In a minute or two, to our chagrin, we stumbled on an outlying spike-bull, evidently kept on the outskirts of the herd by the master bull. I thought it would alarm all the rest; but, as we stood motionless, it could not see clearly what we were. It stood, ran, stood again, gazed at us, and trotted slowly off. We hurried forward as fast as we dared, and with too little care, for we suddenly came in view of two cows. As they raised their heads to look, Woody squatted down where he was, to keep their attention fixed, while I cautiously tried to slip off to one side unobserved. Favored by the neutral tint of my buckskin hunting-shirt, with which my shoes, leggings, and soft hat matched, I succeeded. As soon as I was out of sight, I ran hard and came up to a hillock crested with piñons, behind which I judged I should find the herd. As I approached the crest, their strong, sweet smell smote my nostrils. In another moment I saw the tips of a pair of mighty antlers, and I peered over the crest with my rifle at the ready. Thirty yards off, behind a clump of piñons, stood a huge bull, his head thrown back as he rubbed his shoulders with his horns. There were several cows around him, and one saw me immediately, and took alarm. I fired into the bull's shoulder, inflicting a mortal wound; but he went off, and I raced after him at top speed, firing twice into his flank; then he stopped, very sick, and I broke his neck with a fourth bullet. An elk often hesitates in the first moments of surprise and fright, and does not get really under way for two or three hundred yards; but when once fairly started, he may go several miles, even though mortally wounded; therefore, the hunter, after his first shot, should run forward as fast as he can, and shoot again and again until the quarry drops. In this way many animals that would otherwise be lost are obtained, especially by the man who has a repeating-rifle. Nevertheless the hunter should beware of being led astray by the ease with which he can fire half a dozen shots from his repeater; and he should aim as carefully with each shot as if it were his last. No possible rapidity of fire can atone for habitual carelessness of aim with the first shot.

The elk I thus slew was a giant. His body was the size of the steer's, and his antlers, though not unusually long, were very massive and heavy. He lay in a glade, on the edge of a great cliff. Standing on its brink, we overlooked a most beautiful country, the home of all homes for the elk: a wilderness of mountains, the immense evergreen forest broken by park and glade, by meadow and pasture, by bare hillside and barren table-land. Some five miles off lay the sheet of water known to the old hunters as Spotted Lake; two or three shallow, sedgy places, and spots of geyser formation made pale green blotches on its wind-rippled surface. Far to the southwest, in daring beauty and majesty, the grand domes and lofty spires of the Teton shot into the blue sky. Too sheer for the snow to rest on their sides, it yet filled the rents in their rough flanks, and lay deep between the towering pinnacles of dark rock.

Major Sir Rose Lambert Price
A Summer on the Rockies

Major Sir Rose Lambert Price was born of English royalty, and in some respects he was as pretentious as his name. With inherited wealth he was free to roam the globe sightseeing, hunting, and observing the cultures of unfamiliar peoples.

He had so enjoyed his Nebraska hunting adventure in 1875 that when General John Coppinger invited him to return in 1898 he welcomed the opportunity. Why not? for the General specialized in combining a wilderness experience with all the amenities of civilization. Coppinger saw to it that Price was pampered by his adjutant the moment he disembarked in New York City. Under such circumstances, traveling in America was quite tolerable.

Once in the Teton country, Price joined Dr. Seward Webb's party at his hunting camp a little north of Jackson Lake. In a sense, Webb represented American royalty, for he had married Eliza Osgood Vanderbilt, daughter of Cornelius Vanderbilt. He had plenty of money and believed that it ought to be used to alleviate any hardships for his guests. The chef, Price noted, kept them "a very long way from starvation." A black trooper in the Ninth Cavalry proved "a capital servant. . . ." Champagne was served every night, while 150 men, 113 horses, and 164 mules guaranteed that the seven or so hunters need not be inconvenienced by work.

Before meeting the Webb party, Price, General Coppinger, and a substantial Army contingent made their way up the Wind River from Fort Washakie. They reached the Continental Divide by way of Union Pass, and then enjoined a pleasant descent down the Gros Ventre River. Price's account begins as the party enters Jackson Hole.

ON RISING the hill near the scene of the Smith ambuscade, we got our first view of the Tetons; one of, if not absolutely, the highest range in the Rockies. They suddenly burst on our sight as we topped the hill, and certainly the view was a grand one. They seemed, at the distance we then were from them, to rise out of a great lake, but which was in reality a vast, perfectly grass-covered level plain through which the Snake River ran. The rise was so abrupt that it added greatly to their apparent height, which is 13,654 feet above sea level.

The highest peak in the range—the grand Teton—reminded me somewhat of the Matterhorn, which in some degree it resembles, except that I believe it to be perfectly inaccessible, which the Matterhorn is not. On descending the hill our route lay along the base of the Teton range, with the Snake River running between us, so that we had an uninterrupted view from one end to the other. I noticed with my glasses one considerable glacier, but so placed that I do not think anyone could get up to it.

We were now in the country called Jackson's Hole, and it would be difficult to find a more beautiful one. Immense stretches of prairie land with wild hay growing over it, in many places above one's knees, afforded abundant pasture for cattle. The foothills on each side of the plain are wooded, like the park lands already described, with picturesque clumps of various kinds of timber, interspersed with streams of the clearest and coldest water, well stocked with trout. The various mixture of colours on the hillsides; the light, delicate asparagus green of the quaking aspen; the yellow of the willow, which was just turning; the bright green of the spruce; and the dark green of the pine trees, made a perfect combination. These hills are full of game—elk, black-tail, and antelope—and Mr. Cherry, whose ranche we visited, told me that not less than three thousand elk wintered in them last year. From their sign left on the ground, I am convinced he has not over-estimated the number. All this,

W. Seward Webb hunted big game twice in the northern Jackson Hole country: first in 1896, and then the following year. This F. Jay Haynes photograph shows some of the 1896 party in camp with their kill. The party was so elaborate that soon a taxidermist would be preparing the bull elk heads to adorn the libraries of eastern homes. *Haynes Foundation Collection, Montana Historical Society*

with the magnificent range of the Tetons thrown in, makes Jackson's Hole a very desirable place to live in, and I very much fear it will rapidly settle up.

We pitched our camp this evening on Brush Creek, a beautiful stream of ice-cold water just above Cunningham's ranche, and next morning marched to Cherry's ranche, some fourteen miles from it. Here we had a chapter of accidents. The pack-team and wagons went off in one direction; the General and myself in another; and Perry, and an Indian who had gone to explore our trail, in a third. We all for some time seemed hopelessly lost. The General and myself rode up a steep hill to reconnoitre our position, and Perry, who of all the party alone knew our right directon, caught sight of us and came to the rescue. We soon headed off the wagons and got the outfit on the right trail, and another six miles through a beautiful park-like country brought us to our halting place on a wooded bluff overhanging the Buffalo River, where we formed our permanent camp on the 27th of August, 1897.

• • • • • •

It would be hard to find a more charming spot for a camp than the one we now occupied. Our tents were pitched on a perfectly level piece of ground, about one hundred yards broad by two hundred and fifty long, on a precipitous bluff about sixty feet above the river. Except on the river-side we were completely surrounded and sheltered by a pine forest.

The men had their tents pitched in another open space in the timber, about two hundred yards in our rear, out of sight, but close enough for all practical purposes. From our tents we had an uninterrupted view some twenty miles up the valley of the Buffalo Fork, which has formed by a line of comparatively low, park-like timbered hills on each side of the river, with a broad, flat, willow-covered bottom about a mile across, through which the river would about. At the extreme end of the valley some high mountains ran across it, but so far off as not to cramp the view. The irregularity of the hills on each side, with such a variety of colouring from different shades of foilage, and the open, park-like spaces at intervals all through them, gave an additional charm to the scene; and last, though not least, the ground was covered with any quantity of elk and antelope sign, and the river was full of trout. Along the bottom we found wild geese and duck, and on the hills mountain or blue grouse. The weather was charming, and our lines cast in pleasant places; so we waited with a contented frame of mind for the big game season to open on the 1st of September.

It commenced auspiciously, six antelopes being brought into camp the first day of the season, all being killed in its immediate vicinity. The 3rd of September was a somewhat eventful day in our annals of camp life. Bob Emmet and Bat started with a pack-train of seven mules for a week's hunt, and my feelings at seeing them ride off may be more easily imagined than described; but the accident which prevented my riding from Wa-

shakie had come against me again, and to my bitter disappointment I had to remain in camp, instead of joining in the hunt,
which for months I had looked forward to. "L'homme propose
et Dieu dispose"—I could only grin and bear it. The pack-train,
with Jack Macfarlane, our packmaster, returned the same day to
Washakie. Both parties had a dreary start to commence their
march with, as it rained in torrents all the day.

Some five and twenty or thirty mouths in camp required a
certain amount of filling; and as butchers' shops do not at present exist in Jackson's Hole, and the men required fresh meat, we
had to take whatever we could most easily get hold of. The stag
elk had not yet commenced running, but there were plenty of
hinds, and up to the 8th of September we killed nine antelopes
and eleven elk for meat. On the 10th of September Emmet
returned from his first hunt. He had gone to a line of country
about twenty miles eastward of our camp, chiefly with the
object of hunting for mountain sheep (*ovis montana*) and bears,
but had come across neither. Of sheep he had seen no sign
whatever, and had only struck the trail of one small bear. He
reported the country as being full of elk, but had seen no large
heads among the numerous bands he had met with. He brought
back one nice head with seven points on one side and six on the
other, not heavy, but symmetrical, and had killed two others
right and left; but unfortunately on the edge of a precipice, over
which they had fallen, and in doing so broke both sets of antlers,
and were not worth bringing in.

The country in places was bad travelling. Any amount of
fallen timber, and at one spot they were obliged to cut steps in
the ice with their hunting knives to get across it. His three stags
were got out of a band of hinds and stags, which had fed into a
sort of precipitous *cul de sac*, out of which they could not escape
without passing close to where he and Bat were waiting for
them; but the ground was so rough, that on being shot two out
of the three stags broke their antlers as already mentioned. He
could have killed any amount of hinds, as they passed within
forty yards of him. They counted a hundred and fifty in another
band, but with no good heads among them. The old stags, how-

ever, often get away without being seen, so some might have been there without having been observed. About half-a-dozen young stags were with them.

Last winter was an unusually severe one in the Rockies, and the deer suffered sadly from the cold and starvation. "Beaver Dick," a local hunter, told Bat that he believed that most of the old stags had perished, as the cold set in very shortly after the rutting, and they had not recovered sufficient strength to enable them to resist its severity. Hunger seemed to make the survivors fearless. They flocked by hundreds into the various ranches to get at the hay, and the settlers had hard work with sticks and stones to drive them off. One man found seventy-three in his corral, and took them all alive and afterwards sold them. Round every hay-yard that I saw here, and at Jackson's Hole, there was invariably a strong pale at least ten feet high, to guard against the elk in winter, at which time of the year, should the season be severe, the place simply swarms.

The Yellowstone National Park, which is strictly preserved, is only twenty miles off, and the government do all in their power to see that this preservation is carried out to the strictest letter of the law. On entering the Park, if a visitor has either gun or rifle, it is taken from him, and kept until his return; or if he is going out by some other route, it is sealed up so that he cannot use it. U.S. soldiers also patrol the Park in all directions to see that nothing is destroyed. All these regulations are admirable, and the Park is full of all kinds of game that is never fired at. Unfortunately, however, the winter food for them is both poor and scanty, and severe weather drives them down to the rich and unprotected pastures of Jackson's Hole, where they are at the mercy of anyone who likes to kill them—an easy accomplishment in hard weather.

On the 13th we struck camp and joined Dr. Seward Webb's hunting party, who were settled about two miles from the north end of Jackson's Lake, within a few hundred yards of the Yellowstone Park boundary.

Our route lay down Buffalo Fork until it ran into the Snake River, and then by Smith's and Sergeant and Ray Hamilton's ranches, on the trail into the Park. To surpass, as a hunting ground, the country that lay on both sides of Buffalo Fork would be impossible. The mountains on both sides were timbered to their summits, with any amount of open intervening parks, affording the very best of feeding, while the uneven, broken nature of the ground gave unusual facilities for easy stalking.

The aspen was now beginning to show its autumn tints, and every shade, from lemon to bright orange, dotted the landscape. The rugged Tetons were always before us in the distance, and the air was indescribably clear. The atmosphere on the Rockies is at times quite wonderful. Space becomes almost obliterated, and objects that are in reality fifty miles off look only about fifteen. This was just such a day, and the clearness with which everything showed out made it one to be remembered, for all was very lovely.

At Smith's ranche, while halting for lunch, we met a small detached hunting party from Dr. Webb's outfit, with pack-mules, etc., *en route* to Jenny's Lake, about twenty-five miles from their main camp.

Our trail now ran somewhat parallel to Jackson's Lake, which at intervals we got glimpses of, and the Tetons, which seemed to run directly out of it, looked almost within gunshot. On a site, evidently selected by an artistic and cultured mind, for nothing could exceed the beauty of the view from it, we found the log house of the late Mr. Ray Hamilton, and his either partner or associate, one Sergeant.

The view extended in an unbroken line for some forty miles, taking in the entire Jackson's Hole country, with Jackson's Lake (about twenty miles long) in the foreground. The entire range of the Tetons was embraced in the panorama, along whose base the blue waters of the lake appeared to wash its shores in a comparatively straight line. On the lake's side, from which we viewed it, the various small wooded ranges over which we had marched ran into the water, forming a succession of bays and timbered peninsulas, the irregularities of which were most charmingly picturesque. Several small islands, covered with a foilage of variegated autumn tints, dotted the ultramarine surface of the

Here from a short distance is the Teton Permanent Camp near Jackson Lake. With only a few hunters and many military servants, one can understand why Price so enjoyed Webb's hospitality. *Haynes Foundation Collection, Montana Historical Society*

water, and altogether it formed a picture of surpassing beauty. Comparisons are odious; but, on looking at this scene of enchantment, I wondered if, in my wanderings over the world, I had ever seen anything that surpassed what I then looked at. The Swiss lakes, the Italian lakes, Killarney; lakes in North America, in South America, in Asia, and in Africa all passed in memory's review—many of them beautiful, but not one of them more so than the vision of loveliness that now lay before me.

A certain amount of romance and mystery lent an additional interest to the Hamilton log hut.

Its late owner, a man of birth and education, had elected to bury himself here, away from all touch with the outside world. The individual who lived with him, if only one-half of the accounts I heard were true, must have been one of the most despicable scoundrels unhung. He had cleared out of the country just in time to escape being "lynched." The ill-fated Mr. Hamilton was found drowned, and nobody seemed quite satisfied as to the manner it happened, and all sorts of surmises floated in the air. The furniture in the hut had nearly all been removed, but the few articles left were in perfect keeping with the good taste displayed in the rustic but very pretty interior. Most of our party knew something of, or about, its late unfortunate owner, so a melancholy interest attached itself to the spot, which the accounts of the wickedness perpetrated there after his death by this creature Sergeant seemed to deepen.

A few miles further through the wooded valley of the Snake River brought us to a succession of large grass-covered flats, and on a small backwater of the main river we found our new camp, with the U.S. flag floating gaily in its midst. The two outfits now joined forces, and we all became the guests of Dr. Seward Webb.

The camp, for a hunting party, was an unusually large one, and consisted of 150 men, 113 horses, and 164 mules. The first item embraced the "guns," officers, non-commissioned officers, troopers, civilian employés, enlisted teamsters, packers, Indians, and civilian servants. The tents formed three sides of a large square, with the escort wagons and spring hunting wagons in the centre. The site, though not anything like as convenient or well-chosen as our camp on Buffalo Fork, was picturesque in the extreme. One one side the Tetons rose in all their majesty, the Snake River running at their base. A break in them, more resembling a chasm than the entrance to a trail, fronted our position, and afforded the only way of penetrating an apparently impregnable position that led to the ground, where the local hunters assured us we should find mountain sheep.

On the opposite side a succession of lower mountains, covered with all the variegated foilage of autumnal tints, stretched away until some five and thirty or forty miles off they met the still higher range, where Bat and Emmet had hunted for mountain sheep.

To our north lay the wooded rising country included in the timber reservation attached to the Yellowstone National Park; and to the south the grand alluvial plains of Jackson's Hole, which run for over forty miles on each side of the Snake River, and form the great winter feeding ground for all the elk and antelope for more than a hundred miles on each side of it. The winters in the Park are so severe, all the deer in it are driven by starvation from the sanctuary which it affords on to these plains, where they can be slaughtered literally by thousands.

An effort is being made by some people interested in the preservation of wild animals, to induce the government to add a considerable portion of these winter feeding grounds to the National Park. I hope most sincerely they may succeed, for if they do not it will only be a matter of time for the elk to follow the buffalo and disappear off the face of creation. The Doctor's party consisted of five guns: Dr. Seward Webb, Messrs. Creighton and Louis Webb, Purdy, and Bird. As only Emmet and myself hunted from the General's outfit it brought the guns up to seven, or perhaps I should say rifles, as being certainly the more correct expression.

Of our creature comforts while in camp the Doctor took the greatest possible care. A *chef*, with a couple of assistants, kept us a very long way from starvation, and champagne every night for those who liked it was at any rate a beverage not often to be found in a camping outfit near Jackson's Hole. It was very luxurious and very jolly, but "all hands" were far more intent on hunting than on either eating or drinking, and we were all more or less away on detached hunting parties for days or weeks at a time, when neither *chef* nor champagne was included in our commissariat.

The Doctor started off, with Bat Garnier and Beaver Dick as hunters, the day after we arrived in camp, to look for sheep up the gorge penetrating the Tetons. Years ago I have got sheep on quite comfortable ground, and with very little difficulty; but now they are only to be found on, and in, the most uncompromising places; and the Tetons, rugged, bare, and in places utterly inaccessible, form a very typical ground for these rapidly disappearing animals. Beaver Dick, who had a ranche in the neighbourhood, had, with the assistance of his Indian wife (who was quite as good a hunter as himself) located a band of sheep in the Tetons. The Doctor had "blood in his eye," and was keen on the

Beaver Dick Leigh often acted as guide for Webb and many other early hunting parties. Here he stands (rifle in hand) next to his wife. The black soldiers were members of the 9th cavalry escort, and often acted as servants to the hunters. *Haynes Foundation Collection, Montana Historical Society*

ovis montana. I did not see him again for a fortnight, but I believe he got four of them, and one carried a very good head.

Emmet had a mysterious adventure with one which allowed him to get within twenty yards, and then disappeared like a dissolving veiw. It quite scared Tigee, the Shoshone hunter, who, though a pious-minded Indian, and not given to habitual profanity, declared it was the devil, and seemed quite relieved when he got clear of the locality.

On the 16th of September the wagons we had brought from Fort Washakie were started back empty under the charge of a non-commissioned officer, on the return journey, the General fearing that if they delayed here longer they might get obstructed by snow when crossing the Divide. The weather was lovely, but we had sharp frosts in the early morning, and the water left in a basin one night in my tent was in the morning frozen solid. The entire party were at this time away in different directions from the main camp; some singly, some by twos. There was any amount of transport for whoever required it. Ten, twenty, thirty mules if necessary, with their aparajoes and packers, were always in immediate readiness for whoever required them, with cook, tent, and as much food and drink as suited the individual requirements of the gentleman, or gentlemen, forming the party. Nothing could have been better managed or more complete.

The hunting radius was generally from twenty to forty miles from permanent camp, so that there was any amount of ground for everyone without the slightest bit of crowding or interfering with one another. With regard to game one could hardly go wrong. It was everywhere. The only difficulty was in getting *good* heads, but of elk there was any quantity.

PART THREE

SEEING AND SETTLING
THE COUNTRY

George Bird Grinnell
One Never Tires of Gazing
at the Grand Range

George Bird Grinnell personifed the broad interests and active life of educated, wealthy men of the late nineteenth century. Often concurrently, his career embraced big game hunting, ranching, ethnology, editing, and writing. Furthermore, his knowledge of geology and the natural sciences marked him as one of the nation's first conservationists concerned with the rampant waste of natural resources. From his position as editor of Forest and Stream he crusaded against the wanton destruction of wildlife and habitat.

During his long life Grinnell journeyed often to the West, although he preferred to live in New York City. His first western adventure was in 1870, when as a Yale student he accompanied Othniel Marsh on a paleontology trip to the Badlands. It was the beginning of his long love affair with the wilderness of the West.

The following selection is from Grinnell's diary, written in the field in 1884. He accompanied Arnold Hague, a geologist officially employed to survey Yellowstone's geological wonders and enlarge the earlier work of the Hayden surveys. In their wanderings Hague and Grinnell journeyed south of Yellowstone and into the northern Jackson Hole country.

Occasionally Grinnell's diary is difficult to decipher and sometimes it is devoid of punctuation. Some editing has been necessary, but it is hoped that nothing has been subtracted from Grinnel's obvious delight with his surroundings.

SEPTEMBER 3, 1884. I started before the pack train this morning intending to try to kill some meat. I crossed the Snake River and rode into the timber pushing up the hill as fast as possible. Down timber and marshy spots made my progress rather slow. The character of the vegetation here is entirely different from that on the other side of the divide. The mountain side, among the green timber, is covered with a thick undergrowth of plants from three to ten feet high. Willows grow along very little creeks and in every depression and ravine. All this shows the greater moisture of the western slope of the mountains. Often it was difficult to force one's horse through the underbrush.

At length, after some hard climbing, I reached the upper edge of the timber; timber which had once extended to the summit of the mountain but had long ago been destroyed by fire. By zig-zagging my horse up the steep slope and winding about the low ridges that run out from it, I, at length, reached the summit of a high mountain from which a superb view could be had. The Red Mountain Range cut off the view, but to the northeast the broad valley of the Snake River lay spread out with its winding silver ribbon of a stream. To the southwest was Jackson's lake, a shining sheet of beautiful water dotted with pine-clad islets. Beyond and above the lake rose the superb mass of the Teton Range. From this point almost the whole range was in view: Moran, a gigantic pile with two or three glacier-like masses of ice on its northern face, and then to the southward two or three smaller mountains. Still further south the towering pinnacles of the Three Tetons shoot skyward, reminding one of the Matterhorn. Along the eastern side of Jackson's lake there are extensive park-like meadow lands and then to the eastward are spread low bare ridges over which the fire has swept, now covered with fallen timber. To the southwest or east lies a massive range of mountains which seem low only by comparison with the wonderful height of the Tetons, and in which lies the Continental Divide. . . .

I kept along the side of the hill where it was pretty steep and below me to the left was a wide valley in which there was some green timber. I was riding along looking down in the valley when suddenly my eye caught sight of an animal standing in an open spot, tail toward me. For an instant I thought it was a horse and the idea flashed through my mind that there was a camp down there. Then the animal turned its head and I saw that it was an elk. In a moment I was off my horse and had moved him back into a little clump of pines where he would be fairly hidden, for the white animal would soon catch the eye of the game. Then divesting myself of my spurs I crept back to the ridge. There were two or three elk in the open, a bull and one or two old cows. A number of others could be seen farther off among the timber. I could have killed one or two of them for they were only about 100 yards away, but if I did so, I could only carry the sirloins with me for I had twenty-five miles to go and I did not care to load my horse with meat and wall.

So I waited about in the hope that a calf or a yearling would show itself. While I waited the elk became uneasy. They would run twenty or thirty yards and then stop and look about them. Just then the pinto got lonely and made a noise. The band started and all plunged into the timbers. I could hear them for quite a distance, making the sticks crash as they trotted through the forest, and then I saw them climb the steep hill near the head of the ravine. . . .

For several miles further I kept to the bare burnt hills, seeing a few recent elk tracks, but no more game. Then I came down to the meadows at the head of Jackson's lake and, striking the trail, pushed on after the pack train. In the afternoon I passed a half breed and a boy who were going into the park. The country is perfectly lovely and one never tires of gazing at the grand range toward which we are going. The mountains are so high that they seem close at hand, yet they never seem to come any closer all through the day's march. They are masses of granite almost ivory in hue with gray here and there. They are little blackened by groves of pine timbers or whitened by patches of snow. They are so steep, however, that it is only in the ravines that the snow can cling to them. Elsewhere it slips off or is blown away by the wind. The ice masses on the north side of Moran appear to be true glaciers, though this could only be certainly determined by an examination of the waters that flow out from beneath them.

A prominent feature of Moran which today came into view is a nearly vertical dike of dark rock moving up the side of a granite face where the rock has been cut away. The dike must be 100 feet wide, and reaches from the summit of the mountain down under a snow mass and then rock at its foot and then appears again on the mountain side below and in a direct line with the upper part of the dike. Just south of the snow and the debris appears a dark mass which looks like a part of the dike broken and pushed to one side.

No good view of Jackson's lake is had after leaving the meadows near its head for the trail passes mostly through lowlands and the shores of the lake are covered with timber. Later in the afternoon we turned away from the lake to cut across to the bend of the Snake River. The country is wet with small lakes and meadows. The timber is very fine, much larger than that seen on the other side of the divide. Some of the pines and firs bring from eighteen inches to two feet in diameter. . . .

A little after passing Buffalo Fork I ran across a buck antelope on the Snake River bottom but got no shot at him. The camp is opposite Mt. Moran and the whole superb Teton Range is seen to the best possible advantage. Fishing good here.

September 4, 1884. Thursday. Yesterday afternoon I saw quite a number of white swans on the Snake River and in little ponds and lakes near at hand. The prospector and his partner, who are camped near us, killed one out of a flock of eight.

Hague and I started about 10 o'clock to go over to Leighs lake and get a nearer view of the Teton Range. We forded the stream in which the water was about halfway up to the horses backs, and then attempted to make our way over to the bluffs. We found a brown marsh overgrown with willows and intersected in all directions by muddy sloughs in which a horse might readily enough sink out of sight. It took us two hours of hard work to make our way northward to a point where we could ride out without difficulty onto the hard prairie. . . .

Reaching the bluffs, we rode over toward the range. The country is curiously carved and sculptured by glacial actions and everywhere are to be seen moraine deposits of great extent. The drift is mainly quartzite granite and serpentine with some volcanic rock. Long ridges composed wholly of this drift run out for a distance from the foot of the range and are now bare of timber for the most part, though on some of them the fire has spared many of the pines, and young quaking apsen timber grows on almost all of them. On the main river terrace—the highest one on the west side—are a number of groups of gorgeous timber stands and single trees left standing by themselves. This is very curious. This terrace is essentially a flat plain though occasionally traversed by ancient waterways a few feet below the general surface of the plain and from 100 yards to one half mile broad. In one place on this plain is left an oval mound, regular in shape, its longer axis at right angle to that of the range. It is perhaps three hundred yards in length, and is, I presume, morainal in character. Quite a number of antelope were seen on this plain but they were very wild and there was no opportunity to get a shot at them. . . .

Keeping onto the northwest we passed over a number of the burned ridges hoping to see Jackson's lake, which there runs in close to the foot of Mt. Moran, but we were unsuccessful. Then, turning southwest, we began to look for Leighs lake. Riding over the burnt hills in this direction we saw a great quantity of elk tracks and trails; some made the night before and some since day light. There was no doubt in my mind but that the ridge here was full of trees.

Having passed over a number of ridges we at length reached one a little higher than the rest from which we had a fine view of the south of Jackson's lake. It winds and twists about among its points and islands and sends out long narrow finger-like bays into the hills in a curious way. Hague said that it only needed a few more points to make it look like the Japanese islands. After looking for a while at this and the grand old mountains and searching the hills for elk, we rode off again to the southwest. In a little while we saw Leighs lake from a hilltop, a pretty sheet of water flowing by an outlet to the south into the Snake River. Here we sat down on the hillside and studied the Tetons again before turning back toward camp. One of the most impressive features about them is their nakedness. They are so utterly bare that it adds to their majesty. . . .

On the way home we saw some antelope, and I shot at a running bunch, shooting a little too high. Passing the end of a burnt hill, a blacktail doe jumped out of the brush and ran across in front of us. I jumped off my horse to shoot, but as I did so she went down into a depression and when I was ready I could only see her ears. She ran off down the ravine. . . .

September 5, 1884. Friday. The storm which had been threatening so long broke upon us last night and today it is raining hard. We did not move, but had breakfast at camp. The rain, sometimes mingled with snow, came down with a persistent drip. Stewart and I and the major rigged up a capital shelter and we ate our breakfast very comfortably in a dry place. . . .

The packers went fishing but came in without having had a bite. About 3 o'clock I set up my rod and went up the river from camp. I had only about an hour and a half to fish, as dinner was promised at 4:30 or five. I began casting at the tail of a riffle below which the water was swift and deep. After a few casts I caught a small trout and then a larger one—perhaps weighing half or three quarters of a pound. They were strong, vigorous fish and their eager way of taking the fly was very pleasant to see.

I followed them down the swift water, and had made a long cast out toward the middle of the stream when a huge fish rose to my tail fly, a brown hackle, but missed it. I cast again over the same spot but this time moved my fly more slowly. He rose again and I struck at just the right moment and had him fast. For a moment he seemed too much astonished to do anything, but he soon recovered himself and then ensued the grandest fight that I have ever had with a trout. He threw himself out of water, then struggled under it, throwing himself over and over as if trying to break the line by twisting it. Then followed furious shaking and tugging, and a long, swift, strong, rush. Then another series of shakes and tugs. It took me twenty-four minutes by the watch to land him. I think it was the most exciting struggle I ever took in part in. . . .

Grace Gallatin Seton-Thompson
A Woman Tenderfoot

Grace Gallatin Seton-Thompson, a proper Victorian lady, preferred to summer in Europe rather than the American West. However, when she married Ernest Thompson Seton in 1896, her holidays changed. Seton was a well-established painter, writer and lecturer. His topics included the American Indian, wilderness, animals and nature. He found his material in the American West.

Thus in 1898 Grace followed "Nimrod," as she called her hunter/ husband, to Jackson Hole. Her account is delightful, and although she has difficult moments in unfamiliar surroundings, she is always up to the task. As she says, one must "keep your nerve, grasp it firmly, and look at it closely."

While in northern Jackson Hole she and Ernest lodged at the Cunningham homestead. From that base she ventured out, enchanted by her surroundings and awed by the Tetons. In a primitivist outburst she wrote that "the real life is to be free, to fly over the grassy mountain meadow with never a limitation of fence or house, with the eternal peaks towering around you, terrible in their grandeur and vastness, yet inviting." Fearful yet challenging, vast yet inviting; that was her summation of the mountainous country of northwest Wyoming.

IT WAS about midnight in the end of August when Nimrod and I tumbled off the train at Market Lake, Idaho. Next morning, after a comfortable night's rest at the "hotel," our rubber beds, sleeping bags, saddles, guns, clothing, and ourselves were packed into a covered wagon, drawn by four horses, and we started for Jackson's Hole in charge of a driver who knew the road perfectly. At least that was what he said, so of course he must have known it. But his memory failed him sadly the first day out, which reduced him to the necessity of inquiring of the neighbours. As these were unsociably placed from thirty to fifty miles apart, there were many times when the little blind god of chance ruled our course.

We put up for the night at Rexburgh, after forty long miles of alkali dust. The Mormon religion has sent a thin arm up into that country, and the keeper of the log building he called a hotel was of that faith. The history of our brief stay there belongs properly to the old torture days of the Inquisition, for the Mormon's possessions of living creatures were many, and his wives and children were the least of them.

Another day of dust and long hard miles over gradually rising hills, with the huge mass of the Tetons looming ever nearer, and the next day we climbed the Teton Pass.

There is nothing extraordinary about climbing the Teton Pass—to tell about. We just went up, and then we went down. It took six horses half a day to draw us up the last mile—some twenty thousand seconds of conviction on my part (unexpressed, of course; see side talk) that the next second would find us dashed to everlasting splinters. And it took ten minutes to get us down!

Of the two, I preferred going up. If you have ever climbed a greased pole during Fourth of July festivities in your grandmother's village, you will understand.

When we got to the bottom there was something different. Our driver informed us that in two hours we should be eating dinner at the ranch house in Jackson's Hole, where we expected to stop for a while to recuperate from the past year's hard grind and the past two weeks of travel. This was good news, as it was then five o'clock and our midday meal had been light—despite the abundance of coffee, soggy potatoes, salt pork, wafer slices

Grace Gallatin Seton-Thompson described the fearful crossing of the Snake River by wagon. A little later the Wilson Ferry and Menor's Ferry, shown here, offered a safer, more convenient method. *American Heritage Center, University of Wyoming*

of meat swimming in grease, and evaporated apricots wherein some nice red ants were banqueting.

"We'll just cross the Snake River, and then it'll be plain sailing," he said. Perhaps it was so. I was inexperienced in the West. This was what followed:

Closing the door on the memory of my recent perilous passage, I prepared to be calm inwardly, as I like to think I was outwardly. The Snake River is so named because for every mile it goes ahead it retreats half way alongside to see how well it has been done. I mention this as a pleasing instance of a name that really describes the thing named. But this is after knowledge.

About half past five, we came to a rolling tumbling yellow stream where the road stopped abruptly with a horrid drop into water that covered the hubs of the wheels. The current was strong, and the horses had to struggle hard to gain the opposite bank. I began to thank my patron saint that the Snake River was crossed.

Crossed? Oh, no! A narrow strip of pebbly road, and the high willows suddenly parted to disclose another stream like the last, but a little deeper, a little wider, a little worse. We crossed it. I made no comments.

At the third stream the horses rebelled. There are many things four horses can do on the edge of a wicked looking river to make it uncomfortable, but at last they had to go in, plunging madly, and dragging the wagon into the stream nearly broadside, which made at least one in the party consider the frailty of human contrivances when matched against a raging flood.

Soon there was another stream. I shall not describe it. When we eventually got through it, the driver stopped his horses to rest, wiped his brow, went around the wagon and pulled a few ropes tighter, cut a willow stick and mended his broken whip, gave a hitch to his trousers, and remarked as he started the horses:

"Now, when we get through the Snake River on here a piece, we'll be all right."

"I thought we had been crossing it for the past hour," I was feminine enough to gasp.

"Oh, yes, them's forks of it; but the main stream's on ahead, and it's mighty treacherous, too," was the calm reply.

When we reached the Snake River, there was no doubt that the others were mere forks. Fortunately, Joe Miller and his two sons live on the opposite bank, and make a living by helping people escape destruction from the mighty waters. Two men waved us back from the place where our driver was lashing his horses into the rushing current, and guided us down stream some distance. One of them said:

"This yere ford changes every week, but I reckon you might try here."

We did.

Had my hair been of the dramatic kind that realises situations, it would have turned white in the next ten minutes. The water was over the horses' backs immediately, the wagon box was afloat, and we were being borne rapidly down stream in the boiling seething flood, when the wheels struck a shingly bar which gave the horses a chance to half swing, half plunge. The two men, who were on horseback, each seized one of the leaders, and kept his head pointed for a cut in the bank, the only place where we could get out.

Everything in the wagon was afloat. A leather case with a forty dollar fishing rod stowed snugly inside slipped quietly down stream. I rescued my camera from the same fate just in time. Overshoes, wraps, field glasses, guns were suddenly endowed with motion. Another moment and we should surely have sunk, when the horses, by a supreme effort, managed to scramble on to the bank, but were too exhausted to draw more than half of the wagon after them, so that it was practically on end in the water, our outfit submerged, of course, and ourselves reclining as gracefully as possible on the backs of the seats.

Had anything given away then, there might have been a tragedy. The two men immediately fastened a rope to the tongue of the wagon, and each winding an end around the pommel of his saddle, set his cow pony pulling. Our horses made another effort, and up we came out of the water, wet, storm tossed, but calm. Oh, yes—calm!

After that, earth had no terrors for me; the worst road that we could bump over was but an incident. I was not surprised that it grew dark very soon, and that we blundered on and on for hours in the night until the near wheeler just lay down in the dirt, a dark spot in the dark road, and our driver, after coming back from a tour of inspection on foot, looked worried. I mildly asked if we would soon cross Snake River, but his reply was an admission that he was lost. There was nothing visible but the twinkling stars and a dim outline of the grim Tetons. The prospect was excellent for passing the rest of the night where we were, famished, freezing, and so tired I could hardly speak.

But Nimrod now took command. His first duty, of course, being a man, was to express his opinion of the driver in terms plain and comprehensive; then he loaded his rifle and fired a shot. If there were any mountaineers around, they would understand the signal and answer.

We waited. All was silent as before. Two more horses dropped to the ground. Then he sent another loud report into the darkness. In a few moments we thought we heard a distant shout, then the report of a gun not far away.

Nimrod mounted the only standing horse and went in the direction of the sound. Then followed an interminable silence. I hallooed, but got no answer. The wildest fears for Nimrod's safety tormented me. He had falled into a gully, the horse had thrown him, *he* was lost.

Then I heard a noise and listened eagerly. The driver said it was a coyote howling up on the mountain. At last voices did come to me from out of the blackness, and Nimrod returned with a man and a fresh horse. The man was no other than the owner of the house for which we were searching, and in ten minutes I was drying myself by his fireplace, while his hastily aroused wife was preparing a midnight supper for us.

To this day, I am sure that driver's worst nightmare is when he lives over again the time when he took a tenderfoot and his wife into Jackson's Hole, and, but for the tenderfoot, would have made them stay overnight, wet, famished, frozen, within a stone's throw of the very house for which they were looking.

• • • • • •

"If you want to see elk, you just follow up the road till you strike a trail on the left, up over that hog's back, and that will bring you in a mile or so on to a grassy flat, and in two or three miles more you come to a lake back in the mountains."

Mrs. Cummings, the speaker, was no ordinary woman of Western make. She had been imported from the East by her husband of three years before. She had been 'forelady in a corset factory,' when matrimony had enticed her away, and the thought that walked beside her as she baked, and washed, and fed the calves, was that some day she would go 'back East.' And this in spite of the fact that for those parts she was very comfortable.

Her log house was the largest in the country, barring Captain Jones's, her nearest neighbour, ten miles up at Jackson's Lake, and his was a hotel. Hers could boast of six rooms and two clothes' closets. The ceilings were white muslin to shut off the rafters, the sitting room had wall-paper and a rag carpet, and in one corner was the post-office.

The United States Government Post-office of Deer, Wyoming, took up two compartments of Mrs. Cummings' writing desk, and she was called upon to be postmistress fifteen minutes twice a week, when the small boy, mounted on a tough little pony, happened around with the leather bag which carried the mail to and from Jackson, thirty miles below.

"I'd like some elk meat mighty well for dinner," Mrs Cummings continued, as she leaned against the kitchen door and watched us mount our newly acquired horses, "but you won't find game around here without a guide—Easterners never do."

Nimrod and I started off in joyous mood. The secret of it, the fascination of the wild life, was revealed to me. At last I understood why the birds sing. The glorious exhilaration of the mountains, the feeling that life is a rosy dream, and that all the worry and the fever and the fret of man's making is a mere illusion that has faded away into the past, and is not worth while; that the real life is to be free, to fly over the grassy mountain meadow with never a limitation of fence or house, with the eternal peaks towering around you, terrible in thier grandeur and vastness, yet inviting.

We struck the trail all right, we thought, but it soon disappeared and we had to govern our course by imagination, an uncertain guide at best. We got into dreadful tangles of timber; the country was all strange, and the trees spread over the mountain for miles, so that it was like trying to find the way under a blanket; but we kept on riding our horses over fallen logs and squeezing them between trees, all the time keeping a sharp watch over them, for they were fresh and scary.

Finally, after three hours' hard climbing, we emerged from the forest on to a great bare shoulder of the mountain, from which the whole country around, vast and beautiful, could be seen. We took bearings and tried to locate that lake, and we finally decided that a wooded basin three miles away looked likely to contain it.

In order to get to it, we had to cross a wooded ravine, very steep and torn out by a recent cloudburst. We rode the horses down places that I shudder in remembering, and I had great trouble in keeping away from the front feet of my horse as I led him, especially when there were little gullies that had to be jumped.

It was exciting enough, and hard work, too, every nerve on a tingle and one's heart thumping with the unwonted exercise at that altitude; but oh, the glorious air, the joy of life and motion that was quite unknown to my reception- and theatre-going self in the dim far away East!

We searched for that lake all day, and at nightfall went home confident that we could find it on the morrow.

Mrs. Cummings' smile clearly expressed 'I told you so,' and she remarked as she served supper: "When my husband comes home next week, he will take you where you can find game."

The next morning we again took some lunch in the saddle bag and started for that elusive spot we had christened Cummings' Lake. About three o'clock we found it—a beautiful patch of water in the heart of the forest, nestling like a jewel, back in the mountains.

We picketed the horses at a safe distance, so that they could not be seen or heard from the lake. At one end the shore sloped gradually into the water, and here Nimrod discovered many tracks of elk, a few deer, and one set of black bear. He said the lake was evidently a favourite drinking place, that a band of elk had been coming daily to water, and that, according to their habits, they ought to come again before dusk.

So we concealed ourselves on a little bluff to the right and waited. The sun had begun to cast long lines on the earth, and the little circle of water was already in shadow when Nimrod held up his finger as a warning for silence. We listened. We were so still that the whole world seemed to be holding its breath.

I heard a faint noise as of a snapping branch, then some light thuds along the ground, and to the left of us out of the dark forest, a dainty creature flitted along the trail and playfully splashed into the water. Six others of her sisters followed her, with two little ones, and they were all splashing about in the water like so many sportive mermaids when their lordly master appeared—a fine bull elk who seemed to me, as he sedately approached the edge of the lake, to be nothing but horns.

I shall never forget the picture of this family at home—the quiet lake encircled by forest and towered over by mountains; the gentle graceful creatures full of life playing about in the water, now drinking, now splashing it in cooling showers upon one another; the solicitude of a mother that her young should come to no harm; and then the head of them all proceeding with dignity to bathe with his harem.

Had I to do again what followed, I hope I should act differently. Nimrod was watching them with a rapt expression, quite forgetful of the rifle in his hands, when I, who had never seen anything killed, touched his arm and whispered: "Shoot, shoot now, if you are going to."

The report of the rifle rang out like a cannon. The does fled away as if by magic. The stag tried also to get to shore, but the ball had inflicted a wound which partially paralysed his hindquarters. At the sight of the blood and the big fellow's struggles to get away, the horror of the thing swept over me.

"Oh, kill him, kill him!" I wailed. "Don't let him suffer!"

But here the hunter in Nimrod answered: "If I kill him now, I shall never be able to get him. Wait until he gets out of the water."

The next few seconds, with that struggling thing in the water, seemed an eternity of agony to me. Then another loud band caused the proud head with its weight of antlers to sink to the wet bank never to rise again.

Later, as I dried my tears, I asked Nimrod:

"Where is the place to aim if you want to kill an animal instantly, so that he will not suffer, and never know what hit him?"

"The best place is the shoulder." He showed me the spot on his elk.

"But wouldn't he suffer at all?"

"Well, of course, if you hit him in the brain, he will never know; but that is a very fine shot. Your target is only an inch or two, here between the eye and the ear, and the head moves more than the body. But," he said, "you would not kill an elk after the way you have wept over this one?"

"If—if I were sure he would not suffer, I might kill just one," I said, conscious of my inconsistencies. My woman's soul revolted, and yet I was out West for all the experiences that the life could give me, and I knew, if the chance came just right, that one elk would be sacrificed to that end.

The next day, much to Mrs. Cummings' surprise, we had elk steak, the most delicious of meat when properly cooked. The next few days slipped by. We were always in the open air, riding about in those glorious mountains, and it was the end of the week when a turn of the wheel brought my day.

First, it becomes necessary to confide in you. Fear is a very wicked companion who, since nursery days, had troubled me very little; but when I arrived out West, he was waiting for me, and, so that I need never be without him, he divided himself into a band of little imps.

Each imp had a special duty, and never left me until he had been crushed in silent but terrible combat. There was the imp who did not like to be alone in the mountains, and the imp who was sure he was going to be lost in those wildernesses, and the imp who quaked at the sight of a gun, and the imp who danced a mad fierce dance when on a horse. All these had been conquered, or at least partially reduced to subjection, but the imp who sat on the saddle pommel when there was a ditch or stream to be jumped had hitherto obliged me to dismount and get over the space on foot.

This morning, when we came to a nasty boggy place, with several small water cuts running through it, I obeyed the imp with reluctance. Well, we got over it—Blondey, the imp, and I—with nothing worse than wet feet and shattered nerves.

I attempted to mount, and had one foot in the stirrup and one hand on the pommel, when Blondey started. Like the girl in the song, I could not get up, I could not get down, and although I had hold of the reins, I had no free hand to pull them in tighter, and you may be sure the imp did not help me. Blondey, realising there was something wrong, broke into a wild gallop across country, but I clung on, expecting every moment the saddle would turn, until I got my foot clear from the stirrup. Then I let go just as Blondey was gathering himself together for another ditch.

I was stunned, but escaped any serious hurt. Nimrod was a great deal more undone than I. He had not dared to go fast for fear of making Blondey go faster, and he now came rushing up, with the fear of death upon his face and the most terrible swears on his lips.

Although a good deal shaken, I began to laugh, the combination was so incongruous. Nimrod rarely swears, and was now quite unconscious what his tongue was doing. Upon being assured that all was well, he started after Blondey and soon brought him back to me; but while he was gone the imp and I had a mortal combat.

I did up my hair, rearranged my habit, and, rejecting Nimrod's offer of his quieter horse, remounted Blondey. We all jumped the next ditch, but the shock was too much for the imp in his weakened condition; he tumbled off the pommel, and I have never seen him since.

Our course lay along the hills on the east bank of Snake River that day. We discovered another beautiful sapphire lake in a setting of green hills. Several ducks were gliding over its surface. We watched them, in concealment of course, and we saw a fish hawk capture his dinner. Then we quietly continued along the ridge of a high bluff until we came to an outstretched point, where beneath us lay the Snake Valley with its fickle-minded river winding through.

The sun was just dropping behind the great Tetons, massed in front of us across the valley. We sat on our horses motionless, looking at the peaceful and majestic scene, when out from the shadows on the sandy flats far below us came a dark shadow, and then leisurely another and another. They were elk, two bulls and a doe, grazing placidly in a little meadow surrounded by trees.

We kept as still as statues.

Nimrod said, "There is your chance."

"Yes," I echoed, "here is my chance."

We waited until they passed into the trees again. Then we dismounted. Nimrod handed me the rifle, saying:

"There are seven shots in it. I will stay behind with the horses."

I took the gun without a word and crept down the mountain side, keeping under cover as much as possible. The sunset quiet surrounded me; the deadly quiet of but one idea—to creep upon that elk and kill him—possessed me. That gradual painful drawing nearer to my prey seemed a lifetime. I was conscious of nothing to the right, or to the left of me, only of what I was going to do. There were pine woods and scrub brush and more woods. Then, suddenly, I saw him standing by the river about to drink. I crawled nearer until I was within one hundred and fifty yards of him, when at the snapping of a twig he raised his head with its crown of branching horn. He saw nothing, so turned again to drink.

Now was the time. I crawled a few feet nearer and raised the deadly weapon. The stag turned partly away from me. In another moment he would be gone. I sighted along the metal barrel and a terrible bang went booming through the dim secluded spot. The elk raised his proud, antlered head and looked in my direction. Another shot tore through the air. Without another move the animal dropped where he stood. He lay as still as the stones beside him, and all was quiet again in the twilight.

I sat on the ground where I was and made no attempt to go near him. So that was all. One instant a magnificent breathing thing, the next—nothing.

Death had been so sudden. I had no regret, I had no triumph—just a sort of wonder at what I had done—a surprise that the breath of life could be taken away so easily.

Meanwhile, Nimrod had become alarmed at the long silence, and, tying the horses, had followed me down the mountain. He was nearly down when he heard the shots, and now came rushing up.

"I have done it," I said in a dull tone, pointing at the dark, quiet object on the bank.

"You surely have."

The Cunningham Cabin Homestead, which is still preserved by the National Park Service, served as living quarters for Grace Gallatin Seton-Thompson and "Nimrod" during their elk hunting adventure in northern Jackson Hole. *American Heritage Center, University of Wyoming*

Nimrod paced the distance—it was one hundred and thirty-five yards—as we went up to the elk. How beautiful his coat was, glossy and shaded in browns, and those great horns—eleven points—that did not seem so big now to my eyes.

Nimrod examined the carcass.

"You are an apt pupil," he said. "You put a bullet through his heart and another through his brain."

"Yes," I said; "he never knew what killed him." But I felt no glory in the achievement.

• • • • • •

Have you ever been lost in the mountains?—not the peaceful, cultivated child hills of the Catskills, but in real mountains, where the first outpost of civilisation, a lonely ranch house, is two weeks' travel away, and where that stream on your left is bound for the Pacific Ocean, and that stream on your right over there will, after four thousand miles, find its way into the Atlantic Ocean, and where the air you breathe is twelve thousand feet above those seas? I have.

The situation is naturally one you would not fish out of the grab bag of fate if you could avoid it. When you suddenly find it on your hands, however, there is only thing to do—keep your nerve, grasp it firmly, and look at it closely. If you have a horse and a gun and a cartridge, it is not so bad. I had these, and I had better than all these, I had Nimrod—but only half of Nimrod. The working half was chained up by my fears, for such is the power of a woman. I will explain.

In crossing over the Continental Divide of the Rocky Mountains, we were guests in the pack train of a man who was equally at home in a New York drawing-room or on a Wyoming bear hunt, and he had made mountain travelling a fine art. Besides ourselves, there were the horse wrangler, the cook (of whom you shall hear later), and sixteen horses, and we started from Jackson's Lake for the Big Horn Basin, several hundred miles over the pathless uninhabited mountains.

No one who has not tried it knows how difficult it is for two or three men to keep so many pack animals in line, with no pathway to guide; and once they are started going nicely, it is nothing short of a calamity to stop them, especially when it is necessary to cover a certain number of miles before nightfall in order that they may have feed.

We were on the Pacific side of the Wind River Divide, and must get to the top that night. The horses were travelling nicely up the difficult ascent, so when Nimrod got his feet wet crossing a stream about noon, he and I thought we would just stop and have a little lunch, dry the shoes, and catch up with the pack train in half an hour.

From the minute the last horse vanished out of sight behind a rock, desolation settled upon me. That slender line of living beings somewhere on ahead was the only link between us and civilisation—civilisation which I understood, which was human and touchable—and the awful vastness of those endless peaks, wherein lurked a hundred dangers, and which seemed made but to annihilate me.

Of course, the fire would not burn, and the shoes would not dry. Blondey wandered off and had to be brought back, and it seemed an age before we were again in the saddle, following the trail the animals had made.

But Nimrod was blithe and unconcerned, so I made no sign of the craven soul within me. For an hour or two we followed the trail, urging our horses as much as possible, but the ascent was difficult, and we could not gain on the speed of the pack train. Then the trail was lost in a gully where the animals had gone in every direction to get through.

My nerves were now on the rack of suspense.

Where were they? Surely, we must have passed them! We were on the wrong trail, perhaps going away from them at every step!

The screws of fear grew tighter every moment during the following hours. Nimrod soon found what he considered to be the trail, and we proceeded.

At last we got to the top. No sign of them. I could have screamed aloud; a great wave of soul destroying fear encompassed me—wild black fear. I could not reason it out. We were lost!

Nimrod scoffed at me. The track was still plain, he said; but I could not read the hieroglyphics at my feet, and there was no room in my mind for confidence or hope. Fear filled it all.

There we were with the mighty forces of the insensate world around, so pitiless, so silently cruel, it seemed to my city-bred soul. It was the spot where Nature spread her wonders before us, one tiny spring dividing its waters east and west for the Atlantic and Pacific oceans, for this was the highest point.

We attempted to cross that hateful divide, that at another time might have looked so beautiful, when suddenly Nimrod's horse plunged withers deep in a bog, and in his struggles to get out threw Nimrod head first from the saddle into the mud, where he lay quite still.

I faced the horror of death at that moment. Of course, this was what I had been expecting, but had not been able to put into words. Nimrod killed! My other fears dwindled away before this one, or, rather, it seemed to wrap them in itself, as in a cloak. For an instant I could not move—there alone with a dead or wounded man on that awful mountain top.

But here was an emergency where I could do something besides blindly follow another's lead. I caught the frightened animal as it dashed out of the treacherous place (to be horseless is almost a worse fate than to be wounded), and Nimrod, who was little hurt, quickly recovered and managed to scramble to dry ground, and again into the saddle.

Forcing our tired horses onward, we again found a trail, supposedly the right one, but there was that haunting fear that it was not. For the only signs were the bending of the grass and the occasional rubbing of the trees where the animals had passed. And these might have been done by a band of elk,

It was growing dusk and still no pack train in sight. No criminal on trial for his life could have felt more wretchedly apprehensive than I. At last we came to a stream. Nimrod, who had dismounted to examine more closely, said:

"The trail turns off here, but it is very dim in the grass."

"Where?" I asked, anxiously.

He pointed to the ground. I could make out nothing. "Oh, let us hurry! They must have gone on."

"I think it would be safer to follow these tracks for a time at least, to see where they come out. There are some tracks across the stream there, but they are older and dimmer and might have been made by elk."

"Oh, do go on! Surely the tracks across the stream must be the ones." To go on, on, and hurry, was my one thought, my one cry.

Nimrod yielded. Thus I and my wild fear betrayed the hunter's instinct. We went on for many weary minutes. We lost all tracks. Then Nimrod fired a shot into the air. He would not do it before, because he said we were not lost, and that there was no need for worry—worry, when for hours blind fear had held me in torture!

There was no answer to the shot.

In five minutes he fired again. Then we heard a report, very faint. I would not believe that I had heard it at all. I raised my gun and fired. This time a shot rattled through the branches overhead, unpleasantly near. It was clearly from behind us. We turned, and after another interchange of shots, the cook appeared.

I was too exhausted to be glad, but a feeling of relief glided over me. He led us to the stream where Nimrod had wanted to turn off, and from there we were quickly in camp, very much to our host's relief. I dropped at the foot of a tree, and said nothing for an hour—my companions were men, so I did not have to talk if I could not—then I arose as usual and was ready for supper.

Of course, Nimrod was blamed for not being a better mountaineer. 'He ought to have seen that broken turf by the trail,' or those 'blades of fresh pulled grass in the pine fork.' How could they know that a woman and her fears had hampered him at every step, especially as you see there was no need?

Always regulate your fears according to the situation, and then you will not go into the valley of the shadow of death, when you are only lost in the mountains.

Fanny Kemble Wister
Jackson Hole, Wyoming

Shortly after the turn of the century, Jackson Hole was discovered by a select group of wealthy easterners. They first came to hunt big game, but they soon discovered the pleasures of spending a summer in the wild and remote valley. The dude ranch business was born, featuring a sophisticated primitivist way of life far from the city crowds and summer humidity.

Philadelphian Struthers Burt was one of the first successful dude ranchers, and it was he who wrote Diary of a Dude Rancher *(1924), a classic account of life on a dude ranch. More recently his son, Nathaniel, wrote of his childhood experiences on his father's Bar BC ranch in* Jackson Hole Journal *(1983). However, perhaps the most charming account of dude ranch life came from the pen of Fanny Kemble Wister, the daughter of Owen Wister. Fanny came with her father to the JY Ranch for the summer of 1911. Snuggled at the base of the mountains on the shores of Phelps Lake, the JY was the first dude ranch in the valley, and a wonderful place to spend the summer months. Her love of the valley and the state of Wyoming is soon evident in this preface to her father's diaries.*

IN 1911 my parents took us, their four oldest children, to Jackson Hole, Wyoming, for the summer. First we camped through Yellowstone Park. We had two teams of horses; one wagon was a buckboard with three rows of seats for us, and the other was a wagon for our camp outfit. There were two drivers and a cook. We camped beside the geysers, where the men made the campfire, put up our tents, and sometimes sang "Turkey in the Straw," with words of their own, while cooking supper. Everybody in the West seemed to have read *The Virginian*, and as soon as they heard my father's name would speak to him about it. The guides talked endlessly to him, asking him questions about the old West. It took about a week to get through Yellowstone, and then we drove into Jackson Hole. When we reached the Snake River, we crossed it on Meaner's Ferry, a flat barge pulled across the turbulent deep river on a cable by Mr. Meaner. We paid, I think, fifty cents a team to Mr. Meaner, who had a white beard and lived alone in his log cabin by the river and ran the ferry by himself.

Mr. Meaner had the only vegetable garden in Jackson Hole, and during the rest of the summer we would often ride to call on him and buy his fresh peas—the only fresh vegetables we had. We stayed for three months at the JY Ranch on Phelps Lake, the first dude ranch in Jackson Hole. We four children had a log cabin to ourselves, and our parents had a cabin of their own next to us. Our wooden bunks were filled with pine boughs and covered with the gray blankets that we slept between. Every morning a bucket of hot water was brought to the cabin door by a filthy old man who, we thought, had something permanently wrong with his jaw. At the end of our stay this turned out to be a quid of tobacco that he had kept in his mouth in the same place for months.

The corral the horses spent the day in was across the outlet of the lake from our cabin. Every morning the old wrangler on the ranch rounded up the horses, turned loose overnight to graze, and drove them back over the hill into the corral. Many of the horses wore bells around their necks at night so that by hearing a bell the wrangler would know where to look for the horse. The delicious clanging of these variously toned bells as the horses galloped into the corral woke us up each day. The old wrangler filled us with awe and admiration. We hung around him as much as possible, for we knew he was the real thing. He wore highheeled boots and leather chaps; the handkerchief around his neck was held by drawing the two ends together through a piece of

Fannie Kemble Wister, daughter of Owen, loved the freedom of Wyoming and Jackson Hole. Here she is in her cowgirl outfit, age eleven, enjoying her summer at the JY Ranch. *American Heritage Center, University of Wyoming*

ham bone. He seldom took off his ten-gallon hat. He could do fancy roping that none of us could learn and from outside the corral could rope whichever horse he chose while they were all madly galloping round and round. Often the horse he caught would be too man-shy to let him come near it. Then he would hand me the heavy bridle embossed in silver with Mexican wheelbit and ask me to bridle the horse for him. At last my destiny was fulfilled. With careful carelessness, I walked slowly into the corral.

We ate in the dining-room cabin, next to the kitchen cabin where a cockney English cook converted by the Mormons was in charge. She had a wooden trough filled by a bucket to wash the tin plates and cups in. She had a young daughter about our age at whom she would fly into terrible noisy rages, screaming at her, "I'll knock your blooming 'ead against the blooming wall." Knowing by her tone that "blooming" was a swear word, we could not comprehend it when the words to our Sunday school hymn next winter at home said the "the blooming earth," which everybody sang with pious looks. Food at the ranch was often scanty, being driven 104 miles by team over the mountains from St. Anthony, Idaho. We had many canned tomatoes; and on days when a steer was shot for beef, we would have some of it for supper that night. The rest of it would hang, covered with a bloody canvas, from a tree until we and the flies had eaten it up. We ate dried, smoked, salted bear meat (like dark brown leather) from the year before; fresh elk too tough to chew, shot when the big-game season opened in September; trout caught by my father, who was a skilled dry-fly fisherman. We frequently found dead flies between the flap-jacks at breakfast, and we drank condensed milk.

We all tried to learn dry-fly fishing from my father, but only the oldest of us succeeded. Mostly we rode, I bareback for miles each day. Fording Snake River, loping through the sagebrush with no trail, we went into the foothills as far as our laboring horses could climb. We were not too young to be stunned with admiration by the Tetons, and we loved the acres of wild flowers growing up their slopes—the tremulous Harebell blue and fragile, the Indian Paintbrush bright red, and the pale, elegant Columbine. We were not awed by the wilderness, feeling that the Grand Teton was our own mountain and the most wonderful mountain in the world, and the Snake River the fastest, longest river in America. We could ride all day and never get past the Tetons. When we returned to the ranch in the late afternoon, we would ride up the brief slope and suddenly Phelps Lake would appear in front of us. The mountains encircling it rose abruptly from the water, with Death Canyon at the far end. Often as we hitched our horses to the rail at the main cabin a cow pony was being lassoed in the corral. There was activity at the ranch; our parents were there. It was good to be back.

Once at the JY a so-called chicken hawk was shot by some enthusiast. We never knew who, and the hawk was thrown for dead on the woodpile where we picked him up intending to add his skin to our collection, which consisted mostly of pack rats whose skins had already turned white for the winter. When we found the hawk still alive, glaring in helpless, savage rage at us, we took him to our parents' cabin and gave him to our father. He found out that the bird's wings were not broken and said that he was not a chicken hawk but a mouse hawk, much more rare, which would never have preyed on the flock of about a dozen chickens at the ranch. My father explained that hawks were unusually strong and that he would try to nurse this one back to health by feeding him raw meat and keeping him for us in his cabin. We agreed that if the bird got well he should go free, for hawks can never be tamed. So, many times a day my father fed raw meat to the hawk, which perched resentfully on his wrist, digging the claws into his skin, watching us hostilely while eating. The bird never became friendly, and one day while we were all there he suddenly without effort soared into the air from my father's wrist and disappeared.

We stayed at Jackson Hole until the snow came in late September. The first elk had been shot. We rode far up into the foothills to watch it being skinned and saw the bullets flattened against its shoulder blade. The pack horses were laden with the carcass and led down the mountain.

Dude ranch outings were popular in Jackson Hole in the early part of the century.
Wyoming State Archives, Museums, and Historical Department

At last we had to return East. We could not stand the thought of leaving. What—sleep in a real bed again and see trolley cars? How frightful! No more smell of sagebrush, no more rushing Snake River, no more Grand Teton. Why did we have to go back?

To get to St. Anthony, Idaho, we drove 104 miles on a single-track dirt road all the way, fording the Snake River and crossing the mountain pass. We spent four nights in roadhouses, the only place for travelers to sleep. The first one, the Lee Road House, was still in Jackson Hole. There the walls were papered with ancient yellow newspapers. Then came Canyon Creek, where arriving in the dark we made a treacherous descent down the steep road to a villainous-looking group of cabins and one barn beside a narrow, roaring river at the bottom of a black canyon. Here I slept behind a curtain on the landing of the stairs. The next day we reached Driggs, a town of one street. It had board-walks for sidewalks, false fronts on some of the houses to make them look as if they were two stories high, and saloons with half-length swinging doors at the corners. All the roadhouses lacked plumbing, and at all of them we ate at long tables covered with white oil-cloth. We used to eat from enameled plates and cups, tin forks and spoons, and we sat on backless benches, talking to the other transients. When we got to Victor, we saw some real two-story houses. The last stop of our journey was St. Anthony, where we boarded the train.

In 1912 we returned to Jackson Hole. We were back with a ranch of our own, for my father had bought 160 acres, and we could not drive fast enough to get to it. When we came to the stone marking the boundary between Idaho and Wyoming, we yelled with joy. Every rock, every sage bush, every aspen tree was different and better because it grew in Wyoming. The landscape changed radically. There was no such other state. With condescension we had looked at Utah, Montana, Idaho, but here at last was Wyoming.

That year we brought our youngest brother, who was then three, and our German governess to look after him—surely the first German governess to set foot in Jackson Hole. We also brought our negro houseman from home, who attracted the attention of Westerners who had never seen a colored man. We brought him to help us build our cabin and to cook for us. We were going to live on *our* ranch.

We also brought with us from home our pet black and white Japanese waltzing mouse in a round "butter tin" with wire handle and tight-fitting cover with holes punched in it for air. Her name was Psyche, which we knew to be "Greek Goddess of Beauty" but pronounced by us "Peeshee." I suppose our parents, who gave us permission to take her on our long journey, never knew what her name really was. Peeshee spent the summer waltzing in Jackson Hole.

We stayed at the JY while building our two-story cabin. The whole family worked, and I can remember no outside help at all. Our ranch was on a sagebrush plain not far from the JY, and we moved in before the cabin was finished.

In October, with hideous reluctance, we had to start East; the weather was cold, and there had been snow. To keep Peeshee warm on the long drive, we took turns holding her in her tin on our laps in the buckboard, but by the end of the day somehow we had all had enough of her. Then my father, who was riding, took her as it began to get dark and much colder. He put on the top of the pommel of his Mexican saddle a hot-water bag; on the top of the hot-water bag he balanced Peeshee in her tin. I cannot now imagine how he got the hot water, but Peeshee survived the trip.

Thinking back forty years to our summers in Wyoming, I see that going West in 1885 made my father. Taking us to undomesticated Jackson Hole linked us to his youth, making us in spirit next of kin to the country of his choice.

Frances Judge
Vital Laughter

Frances Judge spent her childhood in Jackson Hole, and like Fannie Wister, she has a positive remembrance of the experience. However, although the setting was the same, her situation was different. While Wister recalled the delightful freedom of life on a dude ranch, Judge writes of life on a hardscrabble homestead. It was a work-filled, insecure world they endured, but one they would not trade. For all the travail, her grandparents found the valley a paradise, dominated by work yet ruled by laughter and love.

This is a story of "Gram" and "Gramps," 1892 pioneers to the valley. Their experiences and their zest for the hard ranching life of Jackson Hole, whether fighting winter, isolation, or mosquitoes, gives a wonderfully accurate portrayal of many of the pioneer settlers of the valley. The physical remains of their labor has largely disappeared but the glorious setting remains. It was a good life that Gram lived. One filled with children, hard work, self sufficiency, and always "vital laughter."

"I DON'T know who they are," Gram would say, "but I wish they were in hell." And she'd put the binoculars back on the sill of the kitchen window and study for a while, with the naked eye, the potential visitors coming along the road that wound down Uhl Hill, through fields, and along our willow lane.

When Gram felt the need of people beyond the ranch, she dropped everything and took off, down country, on horseback or with team and buggy or, if it were winter, on skis that Gramp had made for her. She preferred going to people rather than having them come to her. It was annoying to have guests come to the ranch; they knocked her routine into a cocked hat; they upset her spontaneous plans. But she never suffered from a guilty conscience over upsetting the plans of others. Yet ranchers were glad to see her arrive, if for no other reason than to hear her laugh. She was the only person we three children knew who could laugh a mile. More than once we had heard her laugh move, full and clear, across the wild, wild fields.

She had known sorrow and uncertainty before she came to Jackson Hole. Here she found her heaven and no one was going to make it hell for her if she could help it.

In 1896, when Gram met and married Gramp—a powerful, handsome Dutchman with a quick limp—he was already established on 160 acres in the upper reaches of the Jackson Hole valley in Wyoming. Gramp—John Shive—took up the land, by squatter's right, about 1892. Since no man could outwork him and few even keep up with him, by the time he married Gram and found himself with a ten-year-old stepdaughter, he was doing as well, in ranching, as could be expected in this high valley in the 1890s.

Gram was thirty-nine years old when she married Gramp. She was not beautiful—never had been; she wasn't even pretty. Her body was short, sturdy, compact, and nail-hard. Her ankles were thick. She was high-chested, flat-breasted. Her face was full, her skin well broken into wrinkles. Her nose was short and round—an unusual nose, unlike anyone else's. Her prematurely gray hair came to a widow's peak on a high forehead. Her eyes were large, wide apart, intelligent, mischievous, and a lovely gentian blue.

Her coarsened skin and her white hair made her seem, upon first appearance, much older than Gramp (she was four years his senior), but not for long. Her high spirit, vitality, and rough gaiety could match those of anyone of any age. Because she did things other women did not do, and didn't give a damn, she was envied.

Part of growing up in Jackson Hole was having a horse and plenty of space to ride it.
American Heritage Center, University of Wyoming

Her childhood had been free but not happy. She grew up in a harum-scarum fashion in the gold camp of Bannack, Montana. She was given the name of Lucy Priscilla, but it was second choice. Since she was born on the eighth of May, her mother wanted to call her Eighthy May, but fortunately her father put his foot down.

That she learned to read is a wonder; she never went beyond the first few grades, and life around her was too interesting and too full of work to be varied with reading. Yet she read well, spelled well, and wrote a pleasing hand. But her English sounded as though it had been chopped with an ax, and always sailed out on a high, harsh voice.

In her teens she was inveigled into marriage by an old man. They had two children: a son that died in infancy, and a daughter, Frances—Fannie. The old, old man could not support his family, so Gram divorced him and hired herself out as a ranch hand. She labored in the hayfields and even broke saddle and work horses as a man might do; in fact, not all men could do such work.

When Fannie was six or seven years old, Gram remarried. Her second husband, James Nesbitt, was a young, meticulous, good-looking Irishman. Because he owned a "photographic studio" in Dillon, Montana, he was known as an "artist." His hair lay beautifully curled on his high forehead and he played in the "city" band. With Jim for a husband Lucy Priscilla—Lou—lived, for a few years, the life of a lady—she who was in the habit of riding horseback over the folded hills around Dillon, herding cattle, chasing wild horses, killing rattlesnakes, cursing the prickly pear, loving the smell of sage, open fields, and log barns. This new life must have been stifling, but she probably would have forced herself to remain in fancy harness for the sake of her two daughters, Fannie and little Carrie Maybelle, if her husband had not been a drunkard. When Carrie was three and Fannie thirteen, she divorced Jim Nesbitt and took pride in hating him and whiskey the rest of her long life.

So she was twice widowed—by choice and probably good sense.

SHE worked her way through hard years. And always with her was the sorrow of Fannie's chronic ill health. A year or two after the girl's marriage Fannie died—a tragic invalid. Gram dispelled her sorrow through heavy work; she scattered her grief over the fields and through the mountains—Fannie had been a gentle, lovely girl. Gram all but fought her heartache with her two fists.

At last, being adventuresome, she made her way to the wild, remote Jackson Hole country. Here with John Shive she found her paradise. They and the West were young together, rough and unbounded. Where the rivers of this valley came from and ran to was no concern of Gram's. Who first saw them and the Teton Mountains meant nothing. She knew no curiosity about their past. The rivers and the mountains were here; wasn't that

A wagon moves across the valley in 1913. Homesteading was popular during this era, but seldom profitable. *Howard Schofield Collection, Wilson, Wyoming*

enough? Life began in this valley with her and Gramp, not beyond. The wind and the rain against her and the sun on her head—that was important. And work and laughter. She never lived in the past; there was no name among her ancestors that she pickled, guarded, and talked about with starched pride. She was not even inquisitive about Gramp's ancestors or his past.

They were simple people, Gram and Gramp. Their original buildings, clustered at the far side of the west field, were entirely utilitarian. But when Gramp built his first house, he saw to it that one window opened to the Teton Range. Later he built Gram a bay window from photographer's glass plates discarded by her. This window swept into view her feeble flower garden that was choked by what nature flung into the yard. The garden was enclosed by an elkhorn fence. The antlers had been hilariously and laboriously gathered by Gram and Mother—Carrie—during those first years in Jackson Hole, when Mother was a child. The two would travel horseback up through open wild meadows into the hills back of the ranch, taking Topsy with them—a mare who would stand perfectly still while being piled high with antlers. After two or three had been roped to a pack-saddle, the rest would interlock and cling one to another—a great bleached network of arms.

All the old buildings wore sod roofs. In the spring they were green with foxtail.

And each spring the old house was papered inside with interesting material. Gram would make a trip down country with team and buggy, gathering magazines and newspapers. She was hardly home when they were slapped on the walls, which was always disappointing and frustrating to Mother, who was thirsty for knowledge; she always hoped for a little time to read before the magazines became a part of the house. But Gram could never see the necessity of learning through reading. However, she would condescend to hand the sheets right side up so that Mother could get a page of a story here, a column of an article there. And she gleaned, through opera glasses given her by a dude, what the ceiling had to offer.

But in time the old house was ready to fall in on them, so they were willing to move. Gramp always said, "Wear out the old before using the new." Literally this had been done.

In all the rest of Jackson Hole there was nothing quite so elegant as the new two-story buildings—the Big House and the Little House—built by my father with all of Gram and Gramp's savings and thousands of dollars more. The houses stood on a bare knoll backed by sage-covered hills that rose into mountains and a wilderness of aspen and pine. The knoll commanded a sweeping view of fields cut by the Buffalo River; a view of many-ridged mountains. And jagging the western skyline were the pinnacles of the Teton Range, standing without foothills, as though they had sprung up overnight. Dad was proud of these buildings he had designed and built. But to Gram and Gramp these buildings were no more pleasant than were the old ones in the west field with the elkhorn fence, the bachelor-buttons and weeds in the yard, and hop vines climbing the house logs.

Work was the one significant thing in ranch life. Gram, having the strength of a horse, expected the same strength of everyone else. Everyone had to work. To get ahead of what? Perhaps Mother Nature, perhaps Gram. Gramp was the only one who could keep ahead of both from spring until fall, through winter, and back to spring again.

SPRING! It never came until May. March would be filled with wind, sunshine, snow flurries, and melting icicles—and worry over lack of hay for the stock. April meant hot sun, cold wind, deep snow, more worry over hay, and a restlessness and a longing for spring. It was hell underfoot, as Gram said. The snow was dejected, dirty, porous. One foot went through the crust, the other stayed on top. Damn!

Gram was one of the main reasons we never missed the outside world during those slow months of late winter. Though she ruled us with an exacting hand and tongue and made us do our share of work, she could never hold from us her laughter or her spontaneous fun, and she never tried.

She would come in from outside work looking like the "ragged end of hard times" and pour a cup of coffee. Always the spoon stood in her cup ready to gouge an eye. If Mother and we children were at work in the house, she made our work light with her clowning. She would put down her coffee cup, jump up on a chair, and crow like a rooster or roar like a lion, her eyes big, round, and startlingly blue. Sometimes she drew her skirts tight between her legs and stood on her head for us, against the wall. She could never master this feat without a wall to fall against. We'd howl with laughter and beg, "Do it again, Gram! Do it some more!" If, in our delight, one of us tried to kiss her, she would either hiss like a snake or open her mouth wide so that we'd come within an ace of falling in. She'd say, "You're a bunch of little warriors," and then she'd pretend to swear at us in Chinese, "Afleeuumbaya-a . . . a-eunna-combaya-a. . . ." We never knew whether she made up the Chinese words or had in her childhood heard them in the Montana mining camp. If Gramp happened to be in the kitchen, his face would turn red with his silent laughter. He always enjoyed her raucity.

At table she was funny too. When we had uncooked cabbage at a meal, one or all of us would say, "Oh, be a rabbit, Gram; eat like a rabbit, please!" If she was in the proper mood, she would draw in her cheeks, leaving her lips pinched until they stood up and down, and then she would rabbit-chew. We would sit with our mouths hanging open and watch the cabbage disappear like magic.

Gram's musical entertainment usually came in the evening during that brief period between late chores and early bed. Once in a while she sang for us in Chinese and played her own weird accompaniment on the fiddle. When she played something other than her Chinese specialty, Mother chorded for her on the piano (a small grand that Dad bought Mother when we children were babies), but the accompaniment would be drowned out. When Gram sat at the piano, she played with such gusto that I'm sure the strings vibrated for the rest of the night. Whenever we attended a party at Moran or the Elk schoolhouse or at some ranch, Gram played the banjo or fiddle and called a square dance at the same time, one foot pounding the floor. When she chose the banjo, she always used a nickel as a pick because it made more noise than her fingers could make. Her playing was out of tune, but there was such zip to it no one could keep his feet still. As she said herself, she could play to beat hens a pecking. If she caught the eye of one of us, she would wink as much as to say, "Pretty good, ain't it.?" She'd end a fiddling tune suddenly on a bass note as though she had run amuck and struck something head-on. Once in a great while she played a slow waltz such as "Over the Waves" and it would sound so sorrowful that I would fill with tears. It is probably a good thing her playing was no better than it was or I couldn't have stood it!

When happy, Gram was happy all over; she whistled, laughed, and yelled. When she was mad she was mad all over. When she was sick, she was sick all over—and funny too. She would groan, "I'm going to die. Yes, I'm going to die. Oh, my God, why can't I die?"

She gave herself such drastic treatment for any and all ailments that it is a tribute to her constitution that she lived to be

Joseph Infanger mowing hay on his homestead in 1912. Most of these homesteaders eventually gave up their land or sold out to John D. Rockefeller. Land such as this is now in the National Elk Refuge or in Grand Teton National Park. *Teton County Historical Society*

eighty. Once she put a bit of lye into an aching tooth; the pain almost took off her head—and ours too. She gradually lost her hearing in one ear because she put oil into it that was too hot for the sensitive drum. But Gram, always making the most of any situation, slept with the deaf ear up so as not to be disturbed with night sounds. And her partial deafness brought pleasure to the rest of us in a roundabout way. She would laugh hilariously over amusing things some drab person said to her; someone whom the rest of us had never heard emit a clever word. She would repeat the remarks and we'd all laugh. We finally realized that Gram was laughing over what she *thought* the person said; she never knew that *she* was the clever one.

Once a cow she was milking kicked her in the face, breaking her nose. Gramp and Mother did what they could to repair the damage with the help of a can of Denver Mud. But when the nose was swollen as big as a washtub (it felt that big to Gram), a bee stung her on the chin, swelling it to meet the nose. She looked so tragically funny that no one could keep from laughing. Gram couldn't laugh—there wasn't any place on her face for laughing—but she was a good sport even though she suffered so loud that she could be heard all over the ranch.

One March, when the crusted snow was dangerously glistening, she was struck with snow blindness after a long ski trip. Willingly she took a severe cure, since it was her own idea. Rocks were heated very hot and placed in a tin tub on the floor; Gram was seated on a low chair beside the tub with a heavy blanket thrown over her, tub, and rocks. Slowly sugar was sprinkled on the boulders, sending up a stinging smoke, making the eyes water and burn. Gram wailed and laughed under the blanket, but she lived through the cure. How could her eyes remain their lovely blue?

Gram loved horses. Her love for them was fearless, aggressive, and often took the form of open hostility. Now and again, when she drove a team, the team ran away. Gram would brace her short, thick legs, curse and yell at the horses, and enjoy herself immensely. When she rode Nemo, Mother's dainty chestnut sorrel, the mare ran away, scattering Gram's hairpins over field or hill. However, Nemo never ran away with Mother. She rode the mare with a martingale and checkrein, but Gram couldn't be bothered with a checkrein—she never wore one herself.

Not only could she break horses to ride, but she could also shoe them. However, Gramp never allowed her to do so. He was such a silent man I never knew whether he thought it was unladylike or that Gram might do some damage to the horse.

When Nig died—the co-star of her top buggy team, Nig and Hix—his death brought grief in high comedy. Gram found him dead in the barn one early spring morning; he had gradually wasted away with some horse disease. We all heard her crying as she returned to the kitchen. She didn't want to show weakness, so in the middle of her tears she laughed to herself. She leaned over the stove and actually dripped tears into the huge can of garbage she was heating for the chickens. "Oh, my God, how'll I get on without Nig?" She threw her apron over her face, sat on the arm of a chair, and wailed. Then she laughed for being such a fool over a horse. We gathered around her in sympathy and laughed too, to ease her embarrassment. Ruff, my younger brother, suggested sympathetically that Nig be skinned and the hide tanned, to be hung on a wall somewhere. "Oh, no, no!" she moaned. "I'd just as soon have Jack's hide nailed to the wall as the hide of my favorite horse."

WEATHER in this high country was always interesting. It either hindered or helped crops, livestock, and work. And it was interesting just in itself. Gram would say, "Well, I'll go out and see what the sky has to say." She would brace her sturdy legs, facing the southwest where our storms came from. If it looked like snow she would come into the house saying, "We're going to get more of The Beautiful, damn it." And we always got more of The Beautiful. Damn it.

But May always came, even though Gram was sure it would not. May! The soft air moved one's hair, and the sun brought up good odors from the earth. The bare, lacy aspen branches held an expectant glow. Cattle found a few green things; the hay had lasted or it had not, and that was that.

All winter Gramp kept a pile of manure in the barn so that it would heat. In the spring he would put about four feet of the manure into a very deep pit, top it with four to six inches of rich soil, and cover the whole thing with a glass frame made of photographer's plates which had been carefully saved from the early years when Gram took her first fling at photography. The manure would heat the soil and within three days some of the plants would be up.

All through the long winters we had nothing fresh to eat in the way of vegetables, except cabbage. As soon as the first dandelion greens peeped above the ground in May, Gram would call us and we'd be down on all fours unearthing them. Digging around in the dark, clean soil and smelling the fresh open earth was part of satisfying our hunger. Gram would say, "I know just how a cow feels when she tastes her first spring grass." But soon the dandelions were too big and strong to be palatable, and we hungered afresh for other greens.

But food on the ranch was good. Mother cooked with imagination and beauty and she did most of the cooking, but Gram had a way of putting things together, all her own, that made plain food wonderful. Since she had little respect for reading, she didn't bother much with a cookbook; she made things out of her head. She and Gramp both had a taste for unusual dishes. Every year or two a bear would be killed. The grease—pale yellow and soft like honey—would be used, among other things for deep frying. Gramp was sure that no fat could equal bear grease for doughnuts. And he always carefully skinned and prepared the feet for pickling. What a rare treat—pickled bear's feet!

Other specialties were pickled tongue of elk or pig; the marrow from a fresh boiled bone on delicate bread; hot boiled eggbag, eaten with fresh bread; wild field mushrooms fried in butter (sometimes a dishpanful could be picked from the west field after a gentle rain, but they always had to be gathered young before the worms found them).

The majority of ranchers in Jackson Hole cooked the life out of any kind of meat, so the way Gram and Gramp prepared their elk steaks became known up and down the valley. In our kitchen galvanized pie plates would be heated piping hot in the warming oven while the fire was antagonized with pitch until the top of the stove turned red with heat. T-bone elk steaks were seared quickly on both sides, turned into the pie plates, spread with butter, and eaten immediately. Often they were served with rings of onion sliced into thick sweet cream.

We were very proud of Gramp's cooking. It never failed to be good. And the nearest he ever came to bragging was on his food. He said, "If I have a frying pan with a little flour I kin live a long time in the mountains. But with you kids it's different. You've got to know something. You've got to git an education."

By June the frogs were singing like mad in every pond and there was the voice of killdeer and crane, goose and duck. Cow

About 1900 "Gram" posed with two wolf pups, evidently the survivors of "Gramps'" hunting trips. *Grand Teton National Park*

elk could be heard barking to their calves near the rushing Buffalo River. From the river itself came the grinding sound of uprooted trees that were carried along the swollen current. Snowslides roared like early spring thunder high in the Tetons; we could hear them on warm, dripping days.

The loveliest sign of full spring was the wild clematis trailing from the cow's horn that hung against one wall of the dining room. Busy as Mother was, she would take time to walk to a pine-darkened hill beyond the ranch buildings and bring back the delicate purple flower and its vine. Gram would tramp into the house, drink her coffee with the spoon standing in it, admire the clematis briefly because she loved any and all flowers, and be gone—back to barnyard, hill, or field.

The beastliest sign of June was the mosquitoes. Gram would say, "Oh, my God, the mosquitoes." They whined over and around and through us. They were breathed in. They hung in a cloud over our heads when we stepped outside; they blackened the screen doors. There was no section of Jackson Hole where they were worse. The horses and cattle stamped in anger. We children had bloodstained arms and legs from the bites we scratched. Gram fought the abominable things with her two fists. Sometimes she wore netting over her hat, pulled down, double, to her shoulders. "It won't keep out the damned little things," she once said, "but by doubling it, I befuddle them." Surely, her cursing helped too.

But in spite of mosquitoes and heavy work outdoors, Gram was seldom in trousers. She generally wore a house dress or a shirtwaist with divided skirts—know in Jackson Hole as double-barreled skirts—made of khaki, buttoned or hooked over well-laced corsets. A drive to Jackson, forty miles down country, called for dressing up in fancy shirtwaist and wool skirt with an added piece of jewelry, such as her handmade gold ring set with garnets, or the enormous sterling belt pin covered wtih her curlicued initials—LPS.

The only jewelry Gram wore at home was a pair of small, rough nugget earrings and a heavy gold band on the third finger of her left hand. Until her death, when she was eighty, I took for granted that this wide ring had been placed there by Gramp when they were married. But when the ring came to me I found engraved inside it: *Carrie to Mama, 1902.* Why should Mother give this ring to Gram? Perhaps she was embarrassed because Gram wore no wedding ring. I shall never know the truth.

For Gram and the rest of the grownups summer was a short, warm breath filled with work: haying, seeing to the cattle on the range, repairing fence, washing, ironing, baking—and laughing. The days were longer now, so more work and more laughter could be crammed into the hours between daylight and dark. When haying ended, fall was a swift, bright breath.

And in the fall, hunting for the winter's meat was a natural part of ranch life in the valley. However, any season of the year meant big game hunting for the people of Jackson Hole if they wanted fresh meat, in spite of an established season by the state.

There were guns all through our house; sometimes they stood three deep in a corner. Gramp was the best shot on the ranch, but he took no special pride in it. He hunted methodically, without lust, to get meat we needed. We were sure he couldn't miss an elk if he tried, because one moonlit night in the dead of winter, when a herd of fifty or sixty elk came, in single file, into the north field to pilfer the haystacks that had been fenced away from them, Gramp got up from his bed, took up his gun, and from the bedroom window shot and killed the lead bull. Much to his annoyance he had to get into his clothes, go down into the field, and bleed and dress out the animal so that no meat would be wasted.

Mother was a very good target shot with a six-shooter, but she despised the killing. Gram loved the hunt. Apparently it helped to satisfy the animal in her. Gram's theory was this: If it's fit to eat it ought to be killed; if it ain't fit to eat, it certainly ought to be killed.

When she first came to Jackson Hole she always went big game hunting with Gramp if meat was needed on the ranch. (A rancher, in those days, seldom killed his beef. Cattle were raised to be sold, not to be killed and eaten at home. To bring them successfully to maturity was too expensive and too worrisome for ranch butchering.) Gram would help dress out an elk and drag it home by the saddle horn, or quarter it and bring it in on a pack horse if it were shot any distance from the ranch. Finally she ventured out alone, when meat was needed and Gramp was too busy to go. Within a few hours she returned.

"I got an elk, Jack. A dandy cow."

"Where is it?"

"Why . . . back where I shot it?"

"Did you bleed it? Did you gut it?"

Gram looked sheepish. "I bled it; that's all."

He shook his head. "You've hunted enough with me to know better than that."

"It ain't easy to dress out alone. I thought you'd—"

He cut off her words. "Anybody that shoots an elk around here cleans it and drags it in or they don't go hunting. Go bring in your game."

Gram did as she was told, and though she laughingly cursed Gramp for being no gentleman, she was proud that he made her complete the job. After that she often went alone for meat and brought home the kill.

After the quick brilliant beauty of fall, grass, trees, river, and clouds all moved with the wind, carrying everything into winter. Heavy clouds would shroud the Teton Mountains and, when they lifted, the peaks would be covered with fresh snow. Gram would say, "The mountains are putting on their winter underwear," and shake her head and talk about the gosh-damned wind, and insist that the weather had turned to the devil, and complain about winter coming wrong-end-to. She didn't like winter and she fought it.

But, in truth, she was never held in or down by weather or anything else. She had too many interests and too much work. In winter she carried out her hobbies. Once she decided to study taxidermy. She tried to mount a hawk, but she failed to apply the knowledge she had learned to the whole bird; flies got to the wings—maggots dropped out. The hawk had to be burned. After a little more study, but not enough, she tried to mount a skunk, but the tail wouldn't stand up, it dragged on the floor, so she lost interest in "the art of preparing, stuffing, and mounting the skins of animals in lifelike form."

Photography was of more lasting interest—and far more expensive. Gramp said, in his quiet way, that it took the price of one steer a year to keep her in film and other necessary supplies. She snapped pictures of everyone, coming and going. Usually the clothesline, the woodpile, or the toilet was in the background. Gram had no eye for setting. Or had she? Maybe her goal was to get all three in one picture—clothesline, woodpile, and toilet!

She spent the evenings one winter braiding a fancy horsehair bridle for Mother—sixteen strands. It was professionally done, with tassles hanging all over it and along the braided reins. She always had some other kind of handwork in progress too: paste beads, a melon-seed bag, delicate embroidery. Gram had no eye for color where her clothes were concerned—she might combine green, purple, and red—but the embroidery that lay waiting to be picked up would be white, intricate and expertly done on linen. Now and again, of a winter evening, Gramp would pick up the embroidery and work ten or fifteen minutes, his huge hands dwarfing the piece; yet one could not tell where Gram left off and Gramp began—his work was that well done. How proud we were to think he could brand a calf and embroider with the same two hands! But, of course, Gram could also do both.

We never knew from month to month what her next interest would be. Neither did she.

Gram never wanted Mother to have children, but after we sneaked by her into the world, she was proud of us, though we would never have guessed it by her words. Once when we all got in her way she said to Mother, "Carrie, it's a good thing you didn't have triplets or quadrupeds too or I'd a wrung their damn little necks. If there's anything I hate it's a snarl of kids around." She would fuss about the stringiness of my hair, about Ruff's mouth forever hanging open, and would tell Bill, my twin, that his sharp shoulder blades reminded her of the running gears of a katydid. And she would say to Mother, "My God, Carrie, you don't make these kids eat right and you don't make them comb or wash." Mother, with a week's work piled ahead of her to be done in one day, would only laugh in her light, musical way and tell us what a joy we were to her, what a satisfaction, no matter what we ate or didn't eat, or how we looked. "You are my life," she would say, "I couldn't live without you."

But through Gram's harsh words of ridicule we could feel her pride in us, and read it in her eyes—when we didn't neglect our duties. And we could feel her love for Mother anchored on bedrock, even though she continuously yelled, "Hurry, Carrie, hurry!" as Mother moved slowly through her work. She leaned on the broom or mop and read a magazine until Gram yelled, "My God, hurry!" The handle of the churn slowed down with her reading until Gram screamed, "Hurry, hurry!" She washed and ironed and scrubbed and sang, and though Gram tried to drop a rock into her thoughts, Mother was always mentally free. She could never be chained to scrub pail, broom, churn—or to Gram: she lived an inner life of her own, unrestrained.

And so lived the rest of us.

But Gram was the freest of all. She never tried to be anything but her own unbounded, funny self. Her life was complete. She needed no one from beyond these mountains so long as we all were here. And seldom knowing the need of anyone beyond the ranch, she never ceased wishing her neighbors were in hell—a cheery sort of hell.

For twenty-two years she and Gramp ranched in Jackson Hole. In this valley Gram found her happiness and in this valley she held it.

Work was her life—laced with laughter. And the laughter came easy because the work was good.

PART FOUR

PRESERVING THE BEAUTY

Stephen Leek
The Starving Elk of Wyoming

An attraction of Jackson Hole is the abundant wildlife. For local hunters the game provides food and a challenging hunt, but for most visitors they offer a unique viewing opportunity. In the summer the elk escape to southern Yellowstone and the green-carpeted Thoroughfare country, but as the aspen tree leaves turn and the days grow short they migrate by the thousands to the National Elk Refuge just north of the town of Jackson.

At the turn of the century, however, there was no refuge. Cut off from their normal migration patterns by fences and roads, elk either died of starvation or pilfered ranchers haystacks. It was a pitiful predicament, particularly the winter of 1908–1909 when elk carcasses littered the whole valley. The survivors wandered about desperately seeking nourishment. One pioneer captured the drama through his camera. His name was Stephen N. Leek, and if asked to identify the person most responsible for a winter home for the elk, one would be hard pressed to name a more important individual. Rancher, guide, and wilderness lodge owner, Leek also loved photography, and he used his skills to arouse the conscience of the nation. The following article appeared in the May, 1911 edition of Outdoor Life.

PROBABLY NEVER before in the history of the universe (and I hope never again to be witnessed in the same enormity) has such a sad plight been evidenced among the wild animal kingdom as that which has been witnessed in Jackson's Hole, Wyo. during

Stephen Leek (left) and friend after a successful fishing excursion. *Stephen Leek Collection, American Heritage Center, University of Wyoming*

the past few years. Never until late years have the elk ranges been fenced off like they are now by settlers, and never again, I hope, will the government allow these animals to suffer and die as they have in the past. The late appropriation by Congress and by the state of Wyoming show that the people have at last awakened to the necessity for immediate action—but oh! how long the aid has been a-coming, no one but we who are settlers of the "Hole" and see it with out own eyes every winter can fully realize.

The summer of 1910 was unusually cold and dry, which resulted in a scant growth of grass on the winter range of the elk in Jackson's Hole. An early heavy snowfall in the mountains, with rain in the valley, caused the herds to come down unusually early. This condition prevailed with light snowfall in the valley till about February 15, 1911, when it began storming, and kept it up until the snow was about three feet deep in the valley. Then, turning warmer, it rained for 48 hours, after which it turned colder, snowed some more and finally froze up, effectively shutting the elk from the little remaining grass. For feed they were confined to the willows (two-thirds of which had been killed by the close browsing and peeling to which they were subjectd the two years previous), and to what hay they could steal from the settlers' haystacks.

Before the storm ceased, on February 26th messages were sent to Cheyenne, where the Legislature was in session, calling attention to the need and asking for aid. Four days later we received a reply saying that a bill had passed the House appropriating $5,000 for the relief of the elk. We were further informed that this bill was sure to pass the Senate, and that the Governor would send a man in immediately.

A week later, with no further word from Cheyenne, the calf elk getting very weak and many of them dying, and it being plain to be seen that if any of the calves were to be saved feeding must commence immediately, I sent the following message to several addresses:

JACKSON, Wyo., Feb 7, 1911.—Unless fed, five thousand elk will perish within two weeks. S. N. LEEK.

This might have been putting it pretty strong, but I thought the end justified the means, and in just four days after sending out the message Sheriff Ward of Evanston, Wyo., arrived at Jackson with authority to act, and three days later, February 13, the first load of hay was fed to the elk about one mile north of Jackson. Two days later feeding was commenced on my place, three miles south of Jackson, and on Mr. Kelly's place, one mile farther south.

It was now found that very little hay could be procured in the valley, and Mr. Ward was not authorized to offer a sufficient price for hay to induce or justify any stock to be driven to Idaho. So it was impossible to feed all the elk. Feeding was commenced to about 3,000 head of those in the worst condition, and this has

Elk congregate and joust for position in the newly-established National Elk Refuge. *Stephen Leek Collection, American Heritage Center, University of Wyoming*

Hungry elk forget their fear of man as they approach the hay sleigh on the National Elk Refuge. *Stephen Leek Collection, American Heritage Center, University of Wyoming*

Stephen Leek's photographs of starving elk awakened the consciousness of the nation. *Stephen Leek Collection, American Heritage Center, University of Wyoming*

Following a hard winter the death count was often staggering. *Stephen Leek Collection, American Heritage Center, University of Wyoming*

since been extended to about 5,000 head, though the very limited hay supply (225 tons) makes it necessary to feed barely enough to keep them alive. Feeding was commenced too late to save but very few of the calves, and at this time the hay supply is nearly exhausted. Therefore, if winter does not break soon there will be a very heavy loss yet.

Such, in brief, is the history and situation to date for this year—a repetition of former years. Should I tell you some of the terrible sights we are forced to see—to what extremities the elk are driven for feed or the settlers to save their hay—you would not believe the half of it. But I submit herewith photographs taken on the ground, that will tell more than words.

Nearly the entire calf crop of three years in succession, with many old elk, has perished for want of feed, and including those killed this loss has reduced the magnificent herds of three years ago to less than half their number at that time. As a result we have, in place of young elk coming on, practically all old cows with very few bulls.

The annual report of the ex-State Game Warden for 1910 says: "About the usual number of elk died in Jackson's Hole last winter." I asked Mr. Crawford, an old resident in the valley, and at present feeding the largest bunch of elk being fed, about what percentage of the elk calves died last winter. He said, "80 percent." I next asked Mr. George Wilson, another old resident, the same question. He said, "85 per cent." Mr. Kelly said 75 per cent. The calf crop each year is about 30 per cent of the whole, while there are very few young elk growing up.

It is therefore a fact that we, by permitting this annual normal loss among the elk for want of feed, by allowing one-third or one-half of the calves to perish year after year, are destroying the males only, and making it necessary that the breeding must be done by immature and inferior males, thereby raising degenerate, weak calves that succumb easily to hard winters.

It is necessary in breeding farm stock to select the best sires. In breeding among wild animals nature's intention is to eliminate the weaker, inferior animal, for in their fights during the rutting season the stronger, more mature male drives the others away. In the case of the elk there is not enough mature bulls to go around, and this is causing inter-breeding to some extent, all of which has a tendency to create weak offspring.

Now, the state of Wyoming and the National Government are going to try another experiment—drive the elk like cattle to a better (?) feeding ground. We hope they may succeed, on this proposed new elk range.

Olaus and Margaret Murie
Valley In Discord

Margaret and Olaus Murie came to Jackson Hole in 1927 when Olaus became head of the National Elk Refuge. For some thirty-seven years they participated in the life of the valley, and to this day Margaret (Mardy) remains active in conservation issues.

Conservation has always been a dominant issue. Since the turn of the century, homesteaders, residents, politicians, developers, and federal officials have asked a basic question: "What should we do with this beautiful place?" Like all thoughtful questions, there are no easy answers. After a long struggle the National Park Service laid claim to the mountains when Grand Teton National Park was established in 1929. However, that was just the beginning of land acquisitions. With John D. Rockfeller, Jr.'s money and National Park Service cooperation, much of the private land in the northern part of Jackson Hole was purchased with the intent that this land would become part of an enlarged national park. However, as the Muries explain, this deprivatization of land did not happen easily. Valley residents were divided, creating what the authors term a "valley of discord." Tempers were short, families were often split, and "there was no such thing as getting together and talking it over."

In this essay the Muries capture the flavor of a local feud that had national consequences. When the dust settled what emerged was the pristine park enjoyed by so many today.

OUR CAR begins to take the zigzag turns and we put it into low gear just to be sure. Glancing up the slope, we soon see a piece of the road directly above us, and we know we are approaching the top of Teton Pass. Yes, there is the dip in the ridge just ahead. We leave the hairpin turns, and glide out onto the little flat at the summit.

On every trip over "the Pass" we stop for a bit, and look. Out through the gap fringed with spruce and fir and pine we look into the misty valley far below and see the blue white-flecked mountains beyond. Beside us there is a rustic sign: "Howdy, Stranger. Yonder is Jackson Hole, the last of the Old West."

Those of us who are not strangers, those of us who live down there in the misty blue, will, if we are honest, confess to a little tightening of the throat each time this view bursts upon us. Is that slight mistiness in the scenery, or in our eyes? We don't think so much about "the last of the Old West," but those forest-clad slopes, the very air we breathe, spell HOME.

The valley of Jackson Hole lies here snugly among the mountains that rise on every side. The scenery, the game herds, the wild flowers, the entire ensemble of natural attributes has combined to produce a recreational environment that gives satisfaction and inspiration to hundreds of thousands of people each year. Yet it would seem that the sheer beauty of the place, as it might be with a beautiful woman, has actually been the cause of discord and petty quarreling to a degree almost unique. Neighbor against neighbor, group against group, the feelings have smoldered, leaping out in open conflict from time to time, the bone of contention being: What to do with this beautiful place?

We all praise the memory of that group of frontiersmen of 1870 who in the face of temptation to exploit the Yellowstone region decided to boost for a great national park, the first in the world. But their problem was simpler. They were a small group, and with just a little altruistic feeling among them they could come to a decision. In the 1940's in our valley we were dealing with a situation that had settled into a stubborn groove of tradition.

Yet altruistic impulses were felt in the Jackson Hole country, too, in earlier years. They began with explorers who saw the valley in the previous century. In 1892 Owen Wister wrote: "Of all places in the Rocky Mountains that I know, it is the most beautiful, and, as it lies too high for man to build and prosper, its trees and waters should be kept from man's irresponsible destruction. . . ."

In 1923 there was a notable occurrence, which is commemorated by a bronze plaque at the doorway of a simple log cabin on the banks of Snake River at Moose. The plaque reads:

THE MAUDE NOBLE CABIN

This cabin, erected on its present site in 1917 by Miss Maude Noble, has been preserved and renovated to commemorate a meeting held here on the evening of July 26, 1923, at which Mr. Struthers Burt, Dr. Horace Carncross, Mr. John L. Eynon, Mr. J. R. Jones and Mr. Richard Winger, all residents of Jackson Hole, presented to Mr. Horace Albright, then Superintendent of Yellowstone National Park, a plan for setting aside a portion of Jackson Hole as a National Recreation Area for the use and enjoyment of the people of the United States. The purpose of that plan has been accomplished by the established and enlargement of the Grand Teton National Park.

The broad vision and patriotic foresight of those who met here that July evening in 1923 will be increasingly appreciated by our country with the passing years.

Jackson Hole Preserve, Incorporated

The words on this plaque indicate only the beginning, and the end, of a stormy period in the history of Jackson Hole, a period running from 1918 into the 1950's. The purpose of the meeting at Miss Noble's cabin in 1923 was to devise a means of saving the beauty of the valley from commercial exploitation, from the ruin of its natural beauty; an appeal to have it placed under the supervision of "some public agency." Here is a memorable example of the recognition by a very few people, for the benefit of the future, of the need for safeguarding a meaningful segment of our country from the uses of commerce.

Why the need for such concern, for such an appeal? A simple

Harrison Crandall, one of the finest valley photographers, entitled this work "Winter Solitude in the Tetons." *American Heritage Center, University of Wyoming*

chronology of events will show, I think, what threatened the valley and what human motives were at work in its history:

The years 1918 to 1923 were trying years in Jackson Hole. In 1918 Congressman Mondell introduced a bill for the extension of Yellowstone National Park to include the northern part of Jackson Hole only. Everyone in the valley was opposed to this seemingly thoughtless dumping of a part of the valley into another already large national park. Nevertheless it was twice introduced, and twice failed. During these war years the cattlemen of the valley were able to get good prices; they had visions of expanding their herds and later securing much more of the summer range in the previously created Teton National Forest in the northern and eastern parts of the valley, which at that time had been set apart for the elk herds as the Teton State Game Preserve, under control of the Wyoming State Game Commission. In 1919 the Forest Service began curtailing some use of the ranges by cattle, for the protection of the elk, and this caused angry reactions from cattlemen. Even so, the Park Service, not the Forest Service, was the most hated government bureau. The administration of Yellowstone was suspected of wanting to "swallow up" all of Jackson Hole and do away with cattle ranching and every form of private enterprise. Thus, this early in the play, the Park Service was cast as the villain of the piece.

The tragic flu epidemic of 1918–19 was followed by a severe drought and a short hay crop, but when cattle prices began to tumble after the end of the war, the Jackson Hole ranchers held on, hoping the market would rise, hoping to use more of the valley for cattle ranching; and having had to pay high prices for hay to supplement their own short crops, they found themselves in 1920 bankrupt or heavily in debt or heavily mortgaged by the local bank.

In an attempt to remedy the situation, a few cattlemen made an effort to bring sheep into the valley. Other ranchers and most of the citizens rose in hot protest, and won out, but worry and strife now permeated the clear mountain air.

These were the local events. Added to them were more ominous threats. An engineer in Cheyenne had formed a corporation known as the Teton Irrigation Company and had filed in 1909 and 1912 on the waters of the Gros Ventre River, the Buffalo River, and Spread Creek, the most important Snake River tributaries in the valley. They claimed the purpose of this was to "water" the beautiful sagebrush floor of the valley in front of the Tetons, Antelope Flat, which had been set aside by them under the provisions of a federal law, the Carey Act. But of course the real intention was to sell the water to Idaho farmers, and although the law required the completion of their work in five years, their privilege was extended, by succeeding State Engineers of Wyoming, for a total of twenty-seven years.

In this same unsettled period, through connivance with some local homesteaders, an Idaho corporation known as the Osgood Land and Livestock Company secured an interest in the water-storage rights on two of the valley's lakes, Emma Matilda and Two Ocean. Two years later a citizen of Jackson Hole, in going through some records at the state capitol at Cheyenne, discovered a secret filing by the Carlisle group on the waters of Jenny and Leigh lakes, the two gems at the base of the Tetons themselves.

Here were threats to the natural condition of all the main lakes and streams of the valley, and a threat to the floor of the valley itself. By 1923 the danger seemed very real and ominous to Struthers Burt and his friends who met in Maude Noble's cabin that July evening. They knew that, inexorably, the danger would grow. The water resources of Jackson Hole would be a constant temptation to the acquisitive and the greedy. Owen Wister had been wrong. Jackson Hole did *not* lie "too high for man to build and prosper in." And it now needed to "be kept from man's irresponsible destruction." There were immediate threats to the lakes and streams.

These are reasons for the meeting in Maude Noble's cabin, for the beginning of what was later known as "the Jackson Hole Plan." I have seen the original of a petition requesting preservation of the upper end of Jackson Hole, and on it are the signatures of men who a few years later fought bitterly against establishment of either a national park or a national monument. In 1931, as in 1923, many cattlemen and businessmen were in favor of some kind of preservation plan which would not jeopardize their lives and their business, and the essential purposes of the Jackson Hole Plan were endorsed by the Jackson Hole Cattle and Horse Association. When in 1926 John D. Rockfeller, Jr., became interested and began purchasing ranches and other private lands in upper Jackson Hole with the avowed purpose of later turning them over to the federal government, he was acting on the same motive, but in a practical way. The chronology, however, does not yet become peaceful.

The banker at Jackson was Rockfeller's agent. I talked with him many times, but he was very secretive; in those first days, neither the purchaser nor his plans were disclosed, and this is understandable. I asked the banker if he thought the people of Jackson Hole would be behind the project, whatever it was. He assured me that they would be, and that it "would be a great thing for the valley."

What happened next I shall not attempt to explain. For some reason Rockefeller selected a new purchasing agent. And that changed the whole climate of the valley. From that moment on, the banker and all his associates, many of them cattlemen, were bitterly opposed to the Jackson Hole Plan. They now seemed to see in it the ruin of the cattle business and all freedom of enterprise in Jackson Hole. The plan did not take in the whole valley, but they felt they could not trust the forces behind it; they felt there were Park Service people who wanted everything "rim to rim."

Grand Teton National Park was established in 1929 by mere transfer of National Forest lands covering the mountains and the lakes at the western edge of the valley, which had always been federal lands. The first superintendent of the new national park met the banker on the street in Jackson and was introduced. The banker said: "Well, we fought you as long as we could. You won. Now we will cooperate."

A handsome speech, under the circumstances. One can hardly imagine any substantial number of people, in or out of Wyoming, who would now consider the creation of this park ill-advised. But Rockefeller's program of purchasing private lands in the upper and eastern parts of the valley went on, and opposition to it went on too. As the years passed, it settled into a tradition. The cattlemen became somehow convinced that all their grazing rights would be taken away; the federal government was going to gobble up everything; they had forgotten that quite recently they had petitioned that a great portion of the valley be preserved for recreation and inspiration for all people for all time. As with most feuds, this thing went beyond the state of reasoning for or against a plan; it had become a personal battle, a case of loyalty to one side or to the other. As Dick Winger, the new purchasing agent for Rockefeller, and a resident of the valley since 1913, testified at one of the several Congressional hearings held in Jackson to try to straighten out this controversy: "We don't have clean killings in Jackson Hole; we just worry each other to death!"

Soon after this I got into Dick's car one day to ride home with him. He glanced over at me with a quizzical smile: "Aren't you afraid you'll be condemned now, after being seen riding with me?"

Thus it went on. Jackson Hole might be isolated from the rest of the world in winter, but it always had two burning topics for winter conversation: the elk herd and the park. Card parties, dinner parties had their embarrassments if certain ones prominent on "the other side" were present. In some inexplicable way

Dude ranchers and hunting guides were instrumental in preventing overdevelopment, thus retaining much of the pristine valley that we know today. *Parthenia Stinnett, Teton County Historical Society*

an atmosphere was created in which one felt inhibited from even mentioning the subject. There was no such thing as getting together and talking it over. Congress and our state officials, the federal bureaus, and all the cattle and chamber-of-commerce organizations were concerned, yet through these years it was largely a local feud, a family quarrel. At intervals new rumors drifted up and down the valley. How many more ranches had Rockefeller bought? Was it all going to be added to Yellowstone, or Grand Teton, or what were they going to do with it? Then came a day in March 1943.

I had been up the valley, tramping along the banks of the Gros Ventre River counting dead elk, for March is the month when the weak and sick succumb. As I drove back into town I stopped my car near the post office, and I noticed "Buck," the successor to the former banker, and a real leader in the community, standing in a group of people on the sidewalk. Buck and I were working together in the Boy Scout troop in which his son and our Donald were both members, and I suddenly remembered that I must ask him about the next Court of Honor. I stepped over and began to speak, but didn't get many words said. "Boy Scouts!" he exploded. "Boy Scouts! How can we talk about Boy Scouts now? Haven't you heard what they have done? The President has put our whole valley in a park!"

Thus I received the news that Franklin Roosevelt had, by Executive Order, made a National Monument of all the Rockefeller lands and some remaining federal lands in the east and north parts of the valley. At first I too was stunned. When I came through the back door, Mardy looked up from her mixing bowl: "What's the matter?"

And when I told her, her first reaction was: "But we're in the middle of a *war!* Why do it *now?*"

So we lived through a few more years of battle over the beautiful valley. Bills were introduced in Congress to abolish the Jackson Hole National Monument; more hearings were held in Washington and in the field; the State of Wyoming even brought suit against a superintendent of the Park and Monument, since it would not sue the federal government. Signs appeared in the windows of many business houses: "We are opposed to the Jackson Hole National Monument." A large sign on the outside of one store was partly blown away by a March blizzard, leaving only the word "opposed"—which pretty well expressed the current attitude. If we of the valley, all of us, were to stop now and take a calm look back, I think we might wonder what it was all about. The ranchers of the middle and north parts of the valley had all sold because they wanted to; and yet the other ranchers clung to the idea that their lands and livelihoods were going to be snatched away.

One has to live a dreadfully long time in Jackson Hole to be considered an "Old-timer." I don't think we were considered old-timers even after thirty years of living there. But in spite of this I do think that Mardy and I sensed a bit of how the "real" old-timers, the cattlemen, the long-established townspeople, felt about this "invasion" of their own chosen valley by government, by tourists, by more and more dudes, by proposals to do this or do that with the valley. It is not easy to give up a natural proprietary feeling of ownership and let all the world in. How did the Indians feel at the unheralded arrival of white settlers in land that had always been theirs?

One old-timer, a woman, expressed this feeling rather well when, fourteen years after the establishment of Grant Teton National Park, the bombshell of the Jackson Hole National Monument proclamation dropped into the valley: "We GAVE them the Tetons! What *more* do they want?"

Here is the ubiquitous problem: who is "They"? Grand Teton National Park now includes the Monument lands and nearly all of the lands purchased by Rockefeller, and the noise of battle has died away. Gradually we all have learned to live with it, to recognize the good it holds, to be firm in opposing practices we think bad. We growl about some of the Park Service architecture at the headquarters at Moose, but it at least is limited to one spot. As one drives into and out of the town of Jackson, 14 miles to the south, passing through an unsightly parade of billboards that scar the charming scenery, one cannot help but breathe a sigh of gratitude after crossing the park boundary to find a quiet and serene landscape, marred only by a too-modern highway. It is our park; it is our government; we are they, and they are we. The American public decidedly will not leave this region alone, nor can we ask them to. They will be coming in increasing numbers; it is their country, too.

Now the cattlemen have their grazing rights on the national forest lands, and the right to drift their cattle across national park lands to reach these permits; people still have their homes; dudes still have their summer homes. No one, Old-timer or Newcomer, would now deny that the National Park has vitalized the economy of the valley a thousandfold. These material results are obvious. Our problem now is not the number of acres that are under state or private or federal jurisdiction, but whether or not we can keep most of these acres unspoiled by man; whether or not we can keep our souls receptive to the message of peace these unspoiled acres offer us.

Jackson Hole is not merely a sky-piercing range of mountains for tourists to aim their cameras at. It is a country with a spirit. Grand mountains, to be sure, but also lesser hills harboring on their wooded slopes the bulk of the game herds; a fringe of aspens in the foothills; the sage flats of the valley floor where in primitive times buffalo and antelope grazed; the Snake River bottoms, where white-tailed deer found congenial habitat within the memory of men still living. There is, as one of our neighbors said, "something about it." Those of us who have our homes here and are raising families can help interpret to the visitor the spirit of Jackson Hole, forged out of long controversy, tempered with our love for the valley, for "the something about it."

In our St. John's Hospital in Jackson there is a plaque honoring the parents who donated an operating room to the hospital in memory of their daughter who lost her life in the Tetons, and whose last entry in her diary that long-ago summer had been: "God Bless Wyoming and Keep it Wild."

Fritiof Fryxell
Teton Clouds and Shadows

A great many writers have attempted to describe the Teton mountains. It is difficult to mold the English language to describe such visual grandeur. Perhaps the most successful was Fritiof Fryxell. His background partially explains his success. He earned a master's degree in English from the University of Illinois, and then a Ph.D. in geology at the University of Chicago. It was this education in both literature and science, combined with his love and knowledge of the mountains that provided the tools for exceptional prose.

Fryxell first saw the Tetons in 1924. When the park was established in 1929, he became a ranger-naturalist, spending his summers in Wyoming and the school year teaching geology at Augustana College in Illinois. From June through August he climbed, crawled, scampered, and camped in almost every part of the range, taking scientific and literary notes on his mountain encounters. By 1935 he was ready to write—to distill his experiences. Later, he said, "I hoped to convey as best I could the impression [the mountains] had made on me—both during the first three summers when they served as a 'backdrop' for the valley, and as I got to know them later from traversing the canyons and climbing the peaks."

INTO THE Teton landscape enter many elements which are ceaselessly changing, producing combinations that are new and beautiful. Even the contour of the range undergoes change, as we have observed, but in the large view this is imperceptible, so that seeking permanence in a universe of change we turn to mountains such as these for a symbol of everlastingness.

Over these seemingly changeless mountains, in endless succession, move the ephemeral colors of dawn and sunset and of noon and night, the shadows and the sunlight, the garlands of clouds with which storms adorn the peaks, the misty rain-curtains of afternoon showers. On the range are often set the rainbows; more rarely appears the alpenglow. Along the lower slopes appear the varying shades which the seasons bring to the aspen groves, and in the open meadows unnumbered flowers spring to life and beauty, each for its period and soon replaced by others, perhaps of equal brilliance but of different hues. High above are the snow fields, likewise changing and assuming new patterns as from spring to fall they dwindle, until at last all lose their identity in the mantle of breathless white silence that winter casts upon the region. We see the range now shining with snow, now darkly fearsome in storm, now serene and clean-washed after rain. Always it is changing, yet always it is beautiful.

Early and late in the day the sunlight falls aslant upon the range, throwing its features into strong relief by high lights and shadows. Then it is that the tremendous depth of the chasms is most apparent, as are also the faceted character of the summits and the finer sculptural details everywhere graven in their faces. Then also the range is most awe-inspiring, and yet at the same time it has a mystical, entrancing beauty.

There is no jutting crag or promontory that does not at some hour catch the sun, and at others withdraw into shadow. The shadows are never harsh blacks. They assume pastel shades of blue and purple that run through every conceivable tone, each of which deepens when seen through an opening in the green forest, an optical phenomenon that almost everyone discovers for himself sooner or later.

The hours of early morning or late afternoon provide the best conditions for viewing the Tetons, and there is no better way of seeking a first acquaintance with them than to visit, at these hours, some point far enough distant to afford an unbroken panorama embracing the full sweep of the range, from Buck

Mountain on the south to Eagles Rest and beyond on the north. Deadman's Bar, six miles out on the flats, is one such place often visited, and there are others with much in their favor. If time is very limited, a short stroll out into the sagebrush will suffice to open up a part of the view.

In the middle hours the illumination, being from above, is intense and searching, and falls with too nearly equal value on all the landscape to produce strong contrasts. The shadows on the mountain walls then pale or vanish, the lighting grows severe, and the range assumes an aspect of flatness all out of keeping with its actual rugged relief.

All this the artist knows full well. He also knows that the mirrorlike morning reflections on the lakes are not for the late riser, for as soon as air currents begin to move up the canyons ripples disturb the placid surface of the water. In some respects it is the artist who acquires the clearest understanding of the mountains, for he cannot successfully paint them without first having studied them attentively to learn their varying moods. He it is who is astir with the mountaineer before sunrise, and who a few hours later returns with a canvas that his critic may yawningly dismiss as "overdone" because, having never seen a mountain dawn, he cannot believe that such color effects exist. But whatever the artist's objective or schedule, his paintbox is usually put away from ten in the morning until three in the afternoon, the interval during which colors, shadows, clouds, and reflections are likely to be least impressive.

Late in the afternoon as the sun sinks behind the Teton Range a great shadow moves eastward across the floor of Jackson Hole. Probably few of the thousands who pass through the valley, or even those who spend their lives there, give thought to this daily phenomenon other than to note, perhaps, how the rampart range to the west shortens the length of day in the valley; yet in the perspective that one may gain from the Teton heights the afternoon shadow is a marvelous thing to see, reproducing as it does in silhouette the profile of the range. Unseen, this spectacle has been reënacted daily through the ages; even now few witness it because it takes place at an hour when most hikers and climbers are well on their homeward trek, and already have descended too low. Also, in its swift and soundless course across the valley it may pass unnoticed, for we can be unbelievably oblivious to Nature's offerings, failing to observe unusual cloud displays, celestial phenomena, and the aurora largely because we have the world too much with us even when in the wilderness. Some day the Teton shadow range will become celebrated, and then many will gladly climb the heights to see it, as now they seek them for the sunrise.

I first saw this spectacle in 1929 from near Ramshead Lake, after a late descent from Symmetry Spire. Chancing to glance downward, my attention was riveted by the scene on the valley floor. The shadow peaks of Rockchuck, St. John, and Symmetry Spire were already formed; and from a point a little lower and less obstructed those of Teewinot, the Grand Teton, and Nez Perce came into view (the shadows of Mount Owen and the South Teton merging with those of their forepeaks). At first low and blunt, the shadow peaks lengthened until each had attained its proper relative height, and the full profile was recognizable as that of the familiar Teton skyline. Only for a moment was this so; to have held this picture one would, like Joshua, have had to bid the sun stand still. With increasing distortion and accelerated speed as they were cast more and more obliquely, the shadow peaks pushed onward, crossed the Snake, and, grown to narrow, needle-sharp points, grotesque exaggerations even of peaks as slender as these, raced across the final stretch of Antelope Flats to the far edge of the sagebrush. The Grand Teton shadow was the first to reach it. With all the valley in shade, the peak shadows could still be seen mounting the wooded slopes beyond, but at last these, too, were all obscured, and the phantom range was gone.

Travel to the Tetons is largely confined to the summer season, which at best is brief. In the spring, swift storms continue to whiten the peaks, along the base of which lie persistent snowdrifts that mark the avalanches of the past winter. But one by one the passes are opened, until, by June, from the four points of the compass visitors stream over the mountains into Jackson

Hole. The busy weeks of summer which follow are few and fleeting and, while they last, filled with a beauty so enchanting that time passes unheeded and one is never prepared for the brooding gray days of late August. Then more frequent storms again bring fresh snow to the summits as a prelude to Indian summer, sunset of the year, when one hears in the distance the bugling of the elk, and on the mountainsides sees the aspens turn to gold.

A dweller of the city or lowlands, finding his way to the Tetons at any of these seasons, will discover that here earth and sky meet on terms of undreamed intimacy. Here summits rise aloft to form steps whereby he can literally no less than imaginatively ascend to the very clouds. And here clouds in their turn ofttimes descend to earth, there to re-new association with glaciers and with lakes.

Impressive beyond any telling are those mornings when one awakens to find that in the night clouds have taken possession of the range. Daylight reveals them, poised over the cirques, wreathed about the peaks, or draped in festoons between them, settling into the canyons and trailing slowly along the mountain front. There are days when clouds sink even to the level of Jackson Hole, and with cool, moist fingers touch the tips of the firs, or come to rest over the still lakes. For all that may be seen now, the nearest mountains might be a thousand miles away. Sooner or later the gray curtain rises, and there come into view all up and down the range the gleaming white cascades and waterfalls, each revived and refreshed from the rain that has fallen above.

Many of the summer storms come in the afternoon. As I have have seen them year after year from camps on Jenny Lake, these are brief and dramatic.

Though perhaps foretold several hours by clouds gathering in the range, such a storm almost always breaks with startling suddenness. An arresting sound comes from the west shore, that of the wind bursting from the mouth of Cascade Canyon and encountering the heavy forest. Simultaneously a white line appears on the lake, which advances swiftly. By their agitation the trees on the shore also mark the progress of the storm front. The sound of a gale in the pines is always impressive, and at times alarming. It is sustained like the held notes of cellos in an orchestra, but as the storm approaches there is a crescendo such as no baton ever summoned. Now it sounds in the trees overhead, all about.

The lodgepole pines give proof of their marvelous elasticity. It is remarkable that all are not snapped or uprooted, considering the violence with which they sway and toss. An occasional report does tell of a breaking stem, accounting for broken snags and windfalls throughout the forest—the toll of past storms.

The lake is rising, its surface flecked with white. The first gusts tear the wave crests into sheets of spray. With good reason rowers are cautioned to stay near shore when a storm is imminent, for with wind coming from the canyon like this is a boat in the open might be caught in desperate plight.

Usually rain does not set in at onec. One can stand by the shore for several minutes as onlooker of the pageant in which all Nature takes part. Gradually the agitation of trees and waves becomes more subdued, and when the first big drops strike the water the whitecaps may all have disappeared. From high in the range thunder speaks for the first time, quickly the mountains vanish behind a veil of rain, and the pines straighten, holding out their arms to the rain which now descends in generous measure.

We had come to believe that the wind brought destruction only to the trees that were poorly rooted or otherwise weakened. Then on the stormy night of September 22, 1933, came a blast from Cascade Canyon that swept across the lake and through the forests beyond, felling almost every tree within a quarter-mile strip across the moraine and devastating much of the Jenny Lake campground. Thousands of trees were uprooted or broken, all thrown eastward away from the canyon. Fortunately no one had remained in the camp so late in the season. One large pine fell across and demolished the tent which I, with my wife and little son, had vacated not many days before. The wreckage of the storm was eventually removed, but the forest clearings remain to record a weather caprice such as has oc-

The beauty of Jackson Hole and the Teton Range engendered fierce loyalties and opinions about its fate in the 20th century. *Wyoming State Archives, Museum, and Historical Department*

curred but rarely, if one may judge from the continuity of the forests elsewhere.

A summer of periodic rains is one of few forest fires and, therefore, of freedom from worry on the part of the rangers responsible for the protection of the forests. But occasionally come times of drouth that cause great anxiety, necessitating ceaseless watchfulness and special fire patrols. Each new cloudless day heightens the tension, and as week after week the mountain slopes grow drier and the trails more dusty the menace of fire becomes of grave concern to all.

At such times a thunderstorm may relieve the situation, at least locally, by bringing drenching showers; but if there is little rain the storm may paradoxically make the situation even more critical by leaving in its wake a scattering of fires set by lightning. These, however difficult to reach, must be extinguished at once. So effective is the protection afforded by the ranger staff that no fire within the park has yet gotten out of control, or even assumed serious proportions.

Snow is possible in any month. As a rule the cloud formations that bring it are larger and more formless than others, and linger over the range in a curiously caressing manner.

The snow of summer or early fall comes with a delicate beauty of its own. Perhaps the peaks have long been nearly bare, when one night rain comes to the valley. Because they are mantled with clouds, one knows not the fate of the peaks until at sunrise the mists begin to disperse. Then here and there through cloud rifts are revealed the summits; and behold, they are covered with new snow. It lies on ledges and along the couloirs, emphasizing unsuspected lines in the faces of the most familiar peaks. So white is it that by comparison the shining clouds seem gray. The revelation is brief, for the sun of the new day drives away the clouds, and with them the snow also takes flight. But the scene is imperishably engraved in memory.

Clouds—creatures of sky, to be sure; yet they are thoroughly at home here among the mountains, enjoying close fellowship with peaks and canyons. Large is their contribution to the landscape, adding life and movement to scenes otherwise in eternal repose. When they are absent, the mountains seem austere and bare, and in periods of prolonged drouth one feels vague uneasiness and expectancy. On their return, how unfailing is one's response to their beauty, how eagerly all their movements and changes of form are again followed.

So, for the Teton visitor, clouds and their ways become subjects of absorbing interest.

In the lowlands clouds seem more remote than in reality they are, there being no means of estimating their height. But in the Tetons the range serves as a scale, conveniently graduated as it is with lakes, glaciers, and summits of known elevation.

It is a July day and, high above, a thousand silvery cumuli are silently afloat, casting blue shadows on the slopes and valleys below. As they drift slowly along they clear the highest of the peaks, evidence enough that they must be well over 7,500 feet above our station on the valley floor. But on another day such clouds, possibly larger and darker, less regular of form, are sufficiently low to graze the Grand Teton. They are, then, about 7,000 feet above us and nearly 14,000 feet above the level of the sea. Eventually, as they mass more heavily, they obscure the Three Tetons and Mount Owen, just touching the summit pinnacle of Teewinot. Now they are about 1,500 feet lower than when first observed.

The range not only intercepts the passing clouds; it actually gives birth to many. These are the most fascinating of all. Their forms are legion, and many of their ways devious past finding out, yet one can, with observation, learn much concerning their place and manner of formation.

One type seems fairly obvious. The glaciers and snow fields chill the overlying air so that at times its moisture condenses. On frosty mornings little cloud caps so formed may often be seen, for instance, over Falling Ice Glacier and the east-face snow fields of Teewinot, this despite the general absence of clouds elsewhere. Such clouds are ordinarily short-lived, but if the air is still they may persist for hours.

Other clouds are probably produced by the air currents that encounter the range. Forced sharply upward, these expand and cool. Condensation may occur at various altitudes, depending upon the prevailing conditions of temperature and humidity. When it takes place at low elevations, great cloud banks roll up along the range, and at times blot it from view; when higher, more scattered clouds from here and there among the peaks. As the currents flow along lines predetermined by the contours of the range, they tend to produce clouds at points where they must rise over divides and peaks. Some clouds are best explained in terms of convection, or by the mixing of air from currents of different humidity and temperature.

It is not uncommon to find clouds forming at the very mountaintops. These may linger where formed, may drift some distance away before vanishing, or may be launched in a train miles long, reaching clear across and beyond Jackson Hole.

Teewinot, it has seemed to me, produces the most varied and unusual of clouds. Of many memorable displays, I recall one with special vividness. Late one August afternoon it alone of all the peaks in sight started to form a summit cloud, a solitary formation that grew with extraordinary rapidity, both outward and upward, until in less than half an hour it had become a towering edifice with rounded, glistening white contours, wonderfully smooth and substantial looking. A structure so grandiose could not stand long, and, as I watched, it sank about the summit into shapeless ruins. There was still no other cloud in the range.

Very different was the situation on another August day, suggested in the following note made at the time: "A scene today such as I have not previously observed. At noon when I passed Timbered Island a little cloud cap was hanging over each of the major peaks all the way from Buck Mountain to Eagles Rest. East of the vally were two more, over Jackson Peak and Sheep Mountain. But they were all increasing in size, and an hour or two later, when I again passed this way, nearly all had merged."

Such scenes cannot lose their interest though watched year after year, and references to them crowd my summer journals. To quote a few from one month:

"July 4. Awoke to an overcast sky. Air cool and misty. For several hours this morning the thunder rumbled solemnly over the range (without, however, any distinct peals) as though the peaks were conversing. If peaks could speak, such, I fancy, would be their voices."

"July 11. Storms and sunshine have alternated about the high peaks both yesterday and today with a swiftness almost bewildering."

"July 21. All day clouds have been streaming about among the crags of the near-by peaks, especially St. John, and our handful of visitors have been watching them from the ranger cabin. They have said little, and spoken only in hushed tones of the changing scenes up above, feeling well repaid, I am sure, for the rain and muddy roads they braved to get here. At evening the clouds miraculously dissolved and the summits emerged, fresh and radiant in the sunset."

As was true on that particular July evening, during the hour of sunset the range almost always joins with the heavens in declaring the glory of God, and frequently it happens that of the two the mountains show forth the greater splendor.

For at this time the lofty, richly sculptured north walls of the ridges and peaks one by one emerge from their shadows, even as the other slopes sink into obscurity. Receiving full on their faces the light from the northwest, they take fire, till every crag and pinnacle shines with the brilliance of burnished gold. When the sun passes beneath the horizon this direct illumination is cut off, and now the great precipices assume various colors, crimson, lavender, or rose, whose tones and intensities vary with those in the evening sky from which they are reflected. Slowly, reluctantly, these colors fade from the mountains as they fade from the heavens, but they linger long into the dusk on the very summits on Nez Perce, Teewinot, and others of the high peaks.

Late in the evening, should one stroll down to the lake for a final view of the range, the peak faces might be found still touched with a pale light, as if giving back the last of the radiance received at sunset. But this light, unlike that of a few hours earlier, is silvery and unfading, for it is a light that is shed from the stars. Through the long hours of night it continues, unless extinguished by clouds or, at moonrise, merged in a sudden greater brightness.

Moonlight in its fullest flood brings a spectacle of beauty causing one to abandon every thought of rest, and, heedless of the hour, to set forth anew, as though it were the dawn of day and not its close. For again the features of the range are lighted, but gone now is every trace of austerity, the severeness that by day may frighten or appall. This nocturnal outpouring of light, as revealing almost as day, is infinitely soft and tender, and is deeply fraught with mystery.

No denying fancy now its sway. Are not the peaks grown taller, of nobler stature even than before? Motionless, yet they are alive, these spectral figures, this night met in voiceless conclave for deliberations man may neither share nor comprehend. No matter; enough to be abroad at such a time. And as one starts forth in the night it is with bated breath and cautious step, lest any sound escape and break the reverent silence.

Sources

Langford, Nathaniel. "The Ascent of Mt. Hayden." *Scribner's Monthly* 6 (June 1873): 129–151.

Baillie-Grohman, William A. "Camps in the Teton Basin." In *Camp in the Rockies*. New York: Charles Scribner's Sons, 1882.

Associated Press. "Journey Through the Yellowstone National Park and Northwestern Wyoming, 1883." Associated Press dispatches, Yale University Library, 20–31.

Owen, William. "The Matterhorn of America." *Frank Leslie's Weekly* (May 19, 1892): 268.

Wister, Owen. Diary excerpts in *Owen Wister Out West*. Edited by Fanny Kemble Wister. Chicago: University of Chicago Press, 1958. Permission to reprint has been granted by the University of Chicago Press.

Roosevelt, Theodore. "An Elk-Hunt at Two-Ocean Pass." *Century Magazine* 44 (September 1892): 713–719.

Price, Major Sir Rose Lambert. *A Summer on the Rockies*. London: Sampson Low, Marston & Co., Ltd., 1898.

Grinnell, William Bird. "Through Two Ocean Pass, 1884." Unpublished diary excerpts, Vol. 1, 41–61. Permission to reprint material has been granted by Southwest Museum, Los Angeles, California.

Seton-Thompson, Grace Gallatin. "Outfit and Advice for The-Woman-Who-Goes-Hunting-With-Her-Husband." In *A Woman Tenderfoot*. New York: Doubleday, Page & Co., 1900.

Wister, Fanny Kemble, ed. *Owen Wister Out West*. Chicago: University of Chicago Press, 1958: xiv-xviii. Permission to reprint has been granted by the University of Chicago Press.

Judge, Frances. "Vital Laughter." *The Atlantic Monthly* (July 1954): 47–52. Permission to reprint has been granted by *The Atlantic Monthly* and Frances Judge.

Leek, Stephen N. "The Starving Elk of Wyoming." *Outdoor Life* 27 (May 1911): 441–452.

Murie, Margaret and Olaus. "Valley in Discord." In *Wapiti Wilderness*. Boulder: Colorado Associated University Press, 1985; first edition in 1966. Permission to reprint has been granted by Margaret Murie.

Fryxell, Fritiof. "Teton Clouds and Shadows." In *The Tetons: Interpretations of a Mountain Landscape*. Moose, Wyoming: Grand Teton Natural History Association, 1984; first edition in 1938. Permission to reprint has been granted by the Grand Teton Natural History Association.